Short Cut Cookbook

After taking a course at the School of Domestic Science in Aberdeen, Katie Stewart moved to London to study for a diploma in catering and home management. She took a job with a family in France to perfect her French and then went to the Cordon Bleu school in Paris to take the Cordon Bleu diploma. Back in England she worked as a test supervisor for Nestlé and soon had the opportunity of going to New York, where she learnt about food photography and American foods and methods of cooking, later touring the United States to study regional cookery. On her return to England, Katie Stewart began a career in journalism. She became cookery editor of *Woman's Mirror*, then joined *Woman's Journal*, and was food correspondent of *The Times*. Her writing and her television programmes – practical, funny and refreshingly free of gimmickry – provide her with a very busy working life. She lives in Sussex and has one son.

D1332455

Katie Stewart

Short Cut Cookbook

Pan Books London and Sydney

First published 1979 by The Hamlyn Publishing Group Limited
This edition published in 1981 by Pan Books Ltd,
Cavaye Place, London SW10 9PG
9 8 7 6 5 4 3 2
© Katie Stewart 1981
ISBN 0 330 26507 5
Phototypeset by Input Typesetting Ltd, London SW19 8DR
Printed and bound in Great Britain by Cox & Wyman Ltd, Reading

Contents

Introduction

There are moments in every busy woman's life when the time available for preparing a meal is limited. This calls for quick thinking, good planning and plenty of imagination. It depends on using quick methods of cooking, a sensibly stocked larder and the best use of canned, packet and frozen foods. In fact, short-cut cookery means not so much cooking with less time involved but rather working so that you plan, buy or cook when you have got time, in order to make it easier when you haven't.

Katie Stewart

Kitchen sense

When working against time, it's essential that a kitchen is well planned and organized and that the store cupboard is well stocked. Short-cut cookery does not necessarily demand a huge supply of convenience foods; on the contrary, a clever cook will use them to supplement fresh foods. It does, however, require accurate seasoning, careful use of herbs and spices and attractive presentation in the way of garnishes and decoration.

Every cook should go through her kitchen with care, checking that not only has she got a good selection of equipment, but that the pieces she is most likely to use frequently are placed in the most convenient drawers, cupboards or corners of the kitchen. It's far better to put away all together casseroles or saucepans that are never used, and to keep cutlery drawers filled only with knives and gadgets in daily use. Make sure you have one drawer filled with ready-cut paper liners for tins, kitchen foil, grease-proof paper, polythene bags for storing foods and a roll of cling film wrapping – ideal for covering foods in the refrigerator.

Always prepare a list before you go shopping and stick to it. Meals planned ahead save time and are always more economical – shopping bought in a haphazard manner can be very expensive. Since canned foods keep indefinitely, try over a period of time to build up a sensible and good stock. If the housekeeping allows one week, buy in a few extra cans of food; they may come in handy another week when the budget is tight or time is short. There are many new and interesting products on the market nowadays. Don't be afraid to try something a little unusual. Read all labels carefully before buying to avoid making mistakes.

Kitchen notebooks are great time savers. Keep two, one with tear-out pages to jot down ingredients low in the store cupboard – this way you'll never forget to order foods and won't get caught out for want of an important ingredient, just when you need it most. Attach a pencil with string to the book so members of the family don't keep running off with it! Keep the second book as a recipe collection, and note down ideas of your own or recipes from friends. Take an interest in cooking and swop recipes with other girl friends and stick in ideas you like from magazines.

Spoon measures for speed Many cooks claim that they never measure ingredients at all, but this is a haphazard way of working and any cook who wants to ensure reasonably good results when she is cooking, must measure the ingredients in some way – certainly in all fairness to the recipe she is following. Not all cooks are fortunate enough to have proper weighing scales but spoon measures can be quite accurate enough. Don't use spoon measures for large quantities of liquid. When you are following recipes, however, watch for descriptions of consistency, positions in the oven, cooking times and check that your recipe is following instructions given.

Solid measures

1 rounded tablespoon flour	25 g/1 oz
1 rounded tablespoon soft brown or castor sugar	25 g/1 oz
1 heaped tablespoon icing sugar	25 g/1 oz
2 level tablespoons butter	25 g/1 oz
2 rounded tablespoons grated cheese	25 g/1 oz
1 heaped tablespoon ground almonds	25 g/1 oz
2 heaped tablespoons fresh white breadcrumbs	25 g/1 oz
2 level tablespoons rice	25 g/1 oz
4 level tablespoons rolled oats	25 g/1 oz
3 level tablespoons custard powder, cornflour or cocoa powder	25 g/1 oz
1 level tablespoon powdered gelatine	15 g/½ oz
3 level tablespoons shredded suet	25 g/1 oz
1 heaped tablespoon mixed chopped peel	25 g/1 oz
1 heaped tablespoon currants or sultanas	25 g/1 oz
1 rounded tablespoon syrup	50 g/2 oz
1 rounded tablespoon salt	25 g/1 oz
1 heaped tablespoon semolina	25 g/1 oz
2 rounded tablespoons desiccated coconut	25 g/1 oz

Liquid measures
  2 tablespoons   25 ml/1 fluid oz
  4 tablespoons   60 ml/½ gill
  8 tablespoons   125 ml/¼ pint or 1 gill
  11 tablespoons 175 ml/^{1}/$_3$ pint or 1 teacup

A cook's tools

The best short cuts in all kitchen work come from having the right equipment to work with. Tools may be as simple and necessary as a set of knives, or as specialized as a larding needle or a raised pie mould. Anyone who cooks without the equipment she needs is not only short-handed but much slower.

Knives A minimum number of knives in a kitchen should be one medium-sized knife for chopping, a smaller one for preparing vegetables, a saw-edged knife for breads or cakes, and a sharp, fine knife for carving.

To chop parsley or vegetables finely, always use the heel of the knife. First, using the whole blade, cut the vegetables up coarsely, then chop finely holding the tip of the blade with the left fore-finger and the thumb and with the right hand work the blade up and down very quickly, moving back and forwards over the ingredients. To slice vegetables, keep the tip of the blade on the board, raise and lower the knife handle, slicing as you feed the vegetables under the blade.

Remember, too, that a good sharp kitchen knife will cut delicate cakes far better than a blunt cake knife or a saw-edged knife, especially if the cake is covered or filled with frosting. For a special cake that needs to be cut into neat, attractive slices – perhaps some fabulous dessert or a child's birthday cake – take a confectioner's tip. A warm knife blade softens its way quickly through a frosting or cream and doesn't drag, spoiling the appearance. The easiest way to do this is to fill a jug with hot water, dip the knife blade in to heat for a moment, shake away the drips and then cut the slice quickly. Clean and dip the knife between each cut – sounds like a lot of work but it pays appearance-wise.

Wooden spoons Wooden spoons are best for cooking – they don't scrape or mark the base of a pan and they stand up to high temperatures without getting too hot to hold. There are many different shapes made to get round the edges of pans but the best is the old-fashioned oval spoon. The correct way to stir the contents in a saucepan is to stir once round the sides of the pan then across the middle using a zig-zag movement from side to side, then back round the sides again. Stir continuously like this and you cover the base of the pan to prevent burning and keep the contents moving.

Use wooden spoons for creaming or beating mixtures but never for folding in ingredients. The blunt edge of a wooden spoon tends to knock out air in a light mixture; the cutting edge of a metal spoon is more satisfactory to use. One rubber spatula is handy in a kitchen for cleaning out mixing basins. Treat yourself to at least half a dozen spoons of different sizes – I keep mine, handles down, in a stone jar near the cooker.

Basins and bowls Never skimp on the number of basins and bowls; keep a good selection both large and small. Large bowls are handy for heavy fruit cakes or whipped up mixtures with a good deal of volume and small basins can be used for moulding jellies and desserts or for steaming puddings. To save time when following recipes, measure the volume of your pudding basins with water, then mark it in red nail varnish on the base of each bowl. This same idea could apply to pie dishes and cake tins.

When creaming butter and sugar or when beating eggs and sugar mixtures – cut working time in half by warming the basin first with hot water. Stand the base of the bowl on a damp sponge square or damp corner of a towel, and it won't move while you are working. Hold the basin low – somewhere at hip level – it's less tiring to mix.

Pastry and chopping boards Always keep two boards, a large one for pastry and a smaller one for chopping – both should be at least 2.5 cm/1 in thick. Wood, being a poor conductor of heat, provides a cool, non-slippery surface for working pastry. Best for yeast doughs, too, since the warmed mixture doesn't lose too much temperature from being worked on a very cold surface. When using the chopping board, crush garlic in a corner and use the same one every time. Even after washing, the garlic can flavour other foods prepared on the same board.

Rolling pin The rolling pin used by a professional cook is just a simple straight piece of wood. This is because even pressure on the pin is essential when rolling out pastry or dough for even rising. The palms of the hands should be placed on the pin; roll towards and away from you with quick sharp strokes. The tendency when rolling, if using handles on a pin, is to put too much pressure on the outer edges and not enough in the middle. When rolling out dough, sprinkle flour from a dredger – another valuable piece of kitchen equipment. This way you avoid sprinkling too much flour over the working surface. Remember, too, it's best to flour the pin, never the dough.

A rolling pin is useful for beating out meat thinly – wet the rolling pin and working surface with cold water, then meat won't stick to either.

Hand whisks Different ones are designed, each for a special purpose. A 'balloon' whisk, so named for its shape, is right for beating up egg whites or mixtures needing aerating. The slim plain whisks or the curly-edged variety are marvellous for beating sauces to a smooth consistency. Flat whisks are better for beating batter or pancake mixtures, although I prefer to beat them with a wooden spoon. A rotary hand beater is an invaluable addition to a kitchen although it's not worth dirtying it for very small quantities. Remember that small quantities of ingredients can be whisked together with a fork, and single egg whites come up faster if beaten on a flat plate with a knife.

Kitchen scissors A good pair of kitchen scissors is indispensable – besides using them for the obvious such as snipping, cutting and trimming, let them do difficult chopping tasks as well. Washed herbs or parsley in a teacup can be snipped up finely. Nuts or chocolate, difficult to control with a knife, can be coarsely chopped in minutes using scissors to snip pieces from shelled walnuts or from bars of chocolate. Scissors are ideal for cutting glacé fruits, dates or marshmallows – dip scissors in hot water before each snipping and they won't stick together.

Cooling tray At least two cooling trays should list among kitchen equipment – cakes cool without sweating and pastries or biscuits become crisp when cooled on a wire tray where air circulates around. Newly baked cakes and biscuits are very fragile, so handle carefully – cakes should cool at least five minutes before turning out.

Cooling trays make excellent racks for icing cakes or coating cold, cooked meats and aspic jelly. Place a flat plate underneath, to catch the drips. Spoon over the icing or jelly; any drips or excess mixture which runs into the plate underneath can be returned to the basin and re-used. Leave on the tray until coating has set firm.

Forcing bags and tubes These bags can be used for piping whipped cream, meringue, choux pastry and mashed potato, which make even a simple recipe look more professional. When using the bag, always have the seam on the outside and place in the required nozzle before filling. Fold back a cuff at the top and then spoon in the mixture until three-quarters full, then turn back the cuff and close the bag. One word of warning – never try to pipe a lumpy mixture; this particularly applies to mashed potato. An extra few minutes' beating saves hours of despair.

Flan rings or tart tins A flan ring has no base and should be set on a flat baking tray before use; a tart tin usually has a loose base so that the baked tart can be lifted from the tin. Both are designed for baking pastry cases either with a filling in or for filling afterwards. Once lined with the pastry, to bake the case blind, that is, with no filling, the centre of the unbaked flan must be weighed down in order to keep a flat base. For this, special baking beans, either dried haricot beans, macaroni or rice, may be used if placed on a circle of paper, otherwise crumpled kitchen foil is most suitable. When baking time is almost completed the contents in the centre of the flan and the ring should be gently lifted away and the pastry case returned to the oven to become nice and crisp. The baking beans used should be allowed to cool and then poured into a jar where they are kept only for this purpose.

Best sizes of flan rings to have in a kitchen are 15 cm/6 in flan rings for pies or tarts serving four portions and a 20 cm/8 in ring for larger recipes serving six portions.

Baking tins and trays Any cook's collection of cake and baking tins depends on her interest in baking. Deep round cake tins are best for fruit cakes and the average recipe goes into a 20 cm/8 in round tin; a 25 cm/10 in tin is suitable for Christmas or special occasion cakes. Always have a pair of shallow sponge cake tins, 15–17.5 cm/6–7 in being the average recipe size; if possible a pair of 20 cm/8 in tins as well. Always have two of any size as sponge cakes are most often baked in pairs. For quick reference, mark the sizes in red nail varnish on the sides of the tins. Keep a small and a large loaf tin for quick breads; a 20 or 23 cm/8 or 9 in tube or ring tin; a shallow baking or Swiss roll tin, and possibly a large and a small roasting tin – always useful for baking ginger-breads, or honey cake, besides roasting. Keep at least two, if not more, baking trays – useful for cookies, pies, flans and scones.

When lining cake tins, it's such a waste to cut round paper liners from sheets of greaseproof paper. Use squares of paper for round tins – cut several at a time and keep in kitchen drawer. Remember, as long as two thirds of the base of a round tin is covered the cake will lift out easily. For a square or Swiss roll tin, cut a strip of paper the width of the base and long enough to run up opposite sides of the tin. Loosen unlined sides with a knife before turning out.

Pots and pans Best to buy a set of three or four different-sized, good quality saucepans with lids. A wise cook invests in one small, heavy-based saucepan of excellent quality, possibly cop-per, for making sauces, cooking caramel or other special recipes. Heavy, good quality pans may be tiresome to lift but they cook more evenly and burn far less frequently than thin, cheap pans. A cast-iron frying pan is unbeatable for even frying; often two frying pans will cut down on cooking time. Besides the obvious a frying pan may be used to make a plain or soufflé omelette. Non-stick, silicone-lined pans are super for scrambled egg mixtures which normally stick and take hours of cleaning afterwards. Always wash frying pans after use – store small omelette pans in polythene bags to protect them from the damp atmosphere and dust, and rub a little olive oil into the surface of a cast-iron one. To season a new iron pan, heat about 1 tablespoon oil and plenty of kitchen salt together. Continue to heat until the salt begins to brown – then rub out the inside of the pan with absorbent paper.

Casseroles Pretty oven-to-table casserole dishes speed up serving time considerably. The most useful ones are the heavy, glazed, cast-iron or the new Pyrosil casseroles. Both these may be set over direct heat and can be used for frying, thus cutting out frying pans or saucepans necessary for initial frying for stews or casseroles – this being completed directly in the casserole. Always have one medium-sized and one very large casserole – remember that even for only four servings, recipes calling for four chicken joints, oxtail or other bulky ingredients need space.

Stand casseroles in your roasting tin before putting in the oven; it's easier to remove from the oven when needed and any spilt liquid is saved from burning on the oven floor. Always lightly grease the inside of a casserole with a buttered paper before using – it's much easier to clean out afterwards. If you're serving a meal cooked in the oven-to-table ware, clean away any gravy or cooking stains by rubbing with the damp corner of a teacloth using table salt as an abrasive.

Sieves For most recipes an ordinary wire sieve serves the purpose, whether to sift dry ingredients, purée soups or strain sauces. The old-fashioned hair sieves on a wooden frame are now usually made in nylon with a plastic handle. It's a wise idea to have one of each in a kitchen. When working, it's a good idea to keep one wire sieve always dry, and use it only for sifting dry mixtures, and to use the nylon one for straining liquid ingredients. Nylon sieves are essential for sieving icing sugar or acid fruit or vegetable mixtures, or for any recipe where the wire might discolour or taste the finished recipe.

If ever using a wooden framed sieve, place the shallow side over the basin, leaving the deeper one for recipe ingredients.

Cutters Cutters are not a necessary part of kitchen equipment but, like so many pieces of smaller equipment, add the finishing touches that are important in cookery. Sharp metal cutters are the best – it's a good idea to buy a set with a tin for holding them. When cutting out scones or cookies, spoon a little flour to one side of your working surface and dip the cutter first in the flour each time before cutting the dough. This helps prevent the dough – especially a soft scone dough – from sticking to the cutter. With a plain cutter, press down and twist sharply to one side to make sure the dough is cut, then lift away. With fluted or shaped cutters, press down sharply and firmly but do not twist, otherwise the decorative edge is spoilt.

Food timer Burning or over-cooking wastes time and energy and causes disappointment, too. A timer keeps you up to the minute, and if you're working or sitting in another part of the house, carry it with you, if you're inclined to be forgetful. Best buy is a five-hour timer.

Pressure cooker, food mixer or blender All three undoubtedly save time, in particular the pressure cooker and blender. A food mixer allows you to get on with other jobs while it works, but as with all equipment, work out carefully where it does actually save time and cut down on long tedious jobs before using it. Lengthy cooking of meat, casseroles, soups or puddings makes a pressure cooker invaluable. To blend or purée soups, fruit or fruit drinks takes only a jiffy in the blender, and the tiring whisking of eggs and sugar mixtures, or whipping up gelatine mixtures, can be done with ease on the mixer.

Setting up a store

A clever cook always has a well-stocked store cupboard. Then she's never in a fix for a quick meal or caught out when unexpected guests call. Choose items for the store cupboard carefully and don't buy on the spur of the moment. Once you've mastered a few recipes that can be quickly prepared, see that you always have the necessary ingredients for them in stock. On the other hand, be generous with your collection of dried herbs and seasonings. Keep in plenty of bottled sauces, ketchups and chutneys. Besides the basic food in a store cupboard, never be without such things as mustard, stock cubes, canned tomato purée, oil or vinegar. In glass jars keep plenty of walnuts, flaked almonds, glacé cherries and angelica – many quick desserts depend on a pretty decoration. Savoury recipes depend on an effective garnish – always try to have fresh tomatoes, lemons, onions. Keep parsley in the refrigerator. Buy the nicest bunch of tightly-curled, green parsley you can find. Wash in cold water, shake off all the moisture and place in a polythene bag. Close with a twist tie to exclude the air and keep in the refrigerator. When needed, nip off the curly heads for chopping – this way parsley will keep fresh for four to five days until replaced.

Learn which brands of canned foods you prefer – experiment with different kinds and don't buy, a second time, the ones you dislike. Remember always to wipe the tops of canned foods with a damp cloth before opening – prevents harmful dust from storage contaminating the contents.

Soups Always keep a few cans of cream and condensed or packet soups on hand – they can provide a substantial first course. In summer, tomato soup, vichysoisse or some of the more exotic kinds can be served chilled.

Fish Stock up with two or three cans of sardines in olive oil – they are useful for hors d'oeuvre or salads. Canned tuna fish or salmon are also useful tossed in cold dressings for salads, or for tossing in a well-seasoned, hot parsley or cheese sauce, and they can be served on hot toast with salad as an accompaniment. Cans of shrimps, prawns or anchovies can be used in open sandwiches, for cocktail snacks, as an hors d'oeuvre, in a sauce, over fish or as a filling for vol-au-vent cases. Soft herring roes and pilchards in tomato sauce are useful for snack meals.

Cooked ham, luncheon meat and corned beef These are good buys. They make excellent cold suppers served with new boiled potatoes, tossed in butter and chives, or with cold potato mayonnaise and tossed green salad. Always serve mustard, pickles or chutneys. Slices of pork luncheon meat can be egg-and-breadcrumbed and fried in butter, and sliced ham could be served in a hot parsley or mustard sauce.

Stewed steak, minced beef and frankfurter sausages They can be quickly heated up and, with additions such as fried mushrooms, canned tomatoes, whole carrots or small whole cooked onions, can make the fillings for pies or the basis for casseroles.

Vegetables Always have canned tomatoes in stock – 400 g/14 oz size is the most useful – and small (63 g/2¼ oz size) cans of tomato purée. Both are invaluable for adding flavour to casseroles and many sauces. Cans of small whole carrots or whole new potatoes are excellent for adding to casseroles, celery hearts and butter-beans for snack meals, and whole kernel sweet corn, drained and heated with butter and salt, for a quick vegetable.

Spanish rice, savoury risotto, canned ravioli Topped with plenty of extra grated cheese and browned under the grill these are each delicious served with a tossed salad and hot bread. Add sautéed mushrooms or flaked fish to Spanish rice for extra portions. Canned risotto heated through can be served with grilled sausages or hamburgers.

Cook-in-sauces Cook-in-sauces are useful to have on hand and can be used to produce a casserole or tasty chicken dish with a minimum of effort. To use these, you must appreciate that they are not 'pour over' sauces, nor are they created to be tasted direct from the can. Best results are achieved by cooking meat, fish or poultry in the sauce of your choice. The sauce penetrates the food and enhances the flavour, and the consistency of the sauce does not deteriorate with lengthy cooking time.

Canned fruit, instant whips and puddings These help to make trifles and dessert creams in no time at all and they can be topped with glacé cherries, grated nuts or chocolate. Stock up with fruit jellies and evaporated milk for making a quick mousse; creamed rice and a variety of canned fruits are always useful. Canned apple purée is invaluable to serve as a sauce or dessert, and white peaches are particularly delicious if heated in the oven in their own syrup, with a tablespoon of sherry or brandy.

Keep one or two ready-made pie fillings in stock. One can is usually too small for deep dish pies but excellent for quick plate pies – buy ready-made pastry.

Macaroni, spaghetti and patna rice Always keep plenty since they form the basis for so many meals. Keep a good supply of cheese to accompany pasta dishes. A jar of grated Parmesan cheese stored in the refrigerator comes in handy.

Bread mixes Using a bread mix for home-baked bread and rolls is definitely a saving of time. *White bread* and *brown bread* mixes are available. The 840 g/1 lb 14 oz bags provide sufficient mix to make three medium-sized loaves. The 283 g/10 oz sachets make one medium-sized loaf. The dried yeast in these mixes is very finely powdered and distributed throughout the flour rather in the same way as the raising agent is mixed through self-raising flour. The resulting dough requires kneading for only five minutes and just one proving is necessary to get a good-textured loaf.

You can make a brown cob loaf, a white cottage or a plaited loaf and, of course, you can make rolls from either mix. For added flavour and crunchiness sprinkle loaves or rolls with sesame seeds or cracked wheat before baking. With a little imagination you can adapt the bread dough for use as a pizza base to go along with your favourite savoury topping mix. Store a bread mix in a cool dry place just as you would flour, preferably in the bag with the top folded or twisted down, and remember that it has a shelf life of two weeks once opened. If you have a freezer it could be a sensible use of time and oven heat to batch-bake rolls for packed meals or bread for tea.

Food storage and your refrigerator

A refrigerator is an invaluable asset to any kitchen – besides keeping food clean and fresh, it allows the cook to reorganize her shopping since perishable foods may now be kept longer. Shopping done at off-peak periods is always quickest and easiest, and a busy cook will find her shopping time cut in half if she plans with this in mind.

Obviously, fresh perishable foods cannot be stored indefinitely, the exact time limit depending on how fresh they are when purchased. To save time before shopping, ideas and a list must be carefully worked out. It sounds dull, but if the menus can be roughly planned for each day, not only can you get in all food required, and save last minute shopping, but you can also plan the work so that you can prepare as much as possible beforehand, when you have the time.

Casseroles can be made in advance, or sauces prepared ahead and covered. If you plan on using pastry several times, make it all at once and leave the surplus in a polythene bag in the refrigerator. Actually it makes better pastry than freshly rubbed-in mixtures, because it's nice and cool. Vegetables, salads, fruit desserts or a creamy gâteau can be prepared a day ahead for dinner parties and will keep perfectly.

All food stored in the refrigerator must be protected properly since the action of refrigeration actually draws moisture. Flavours of different foods in the refrigerator will not be absorbed by each other if they are stored in containers or kept wrapped or covered. For this reason, always have rolls of kitchen foil, waxed wrapper paper (greaseproof paper is no use because it is absorbent and allows evaporation to take place) and cling film wrapping. The latter is very handy for placing over cut surfaces of cakes, cheese or fresh fruit as the fine surface of the paper clings to the surface on which it is placed. Plenty of plastic containers, with air-tight lids, and polythene bags are useful too.

Milk and cream Wipe bottles clean and put in the space provided. Milk will keep perfectly fresh for three or four days or even longer in the sealed bottles. Dairy cream will keep for two or three days; if the top of the bottle or carton is broken, cover with an extra piece of foil – cream will absorb other flavours quickly. Commercial soured cream, which is very useful for making sauces for cold meats and salads in summer, will keep up to a week; so will yoghurt – fruit-flavoured ones are useful to keep in the refrigerator for desserts.

Butter and cooking fats Leave in original wrapping – this gives sufficient protection. Butter will keep up to a week, and this applies to all cooking fats. Suet or clarified dripping will keep almost indefinitely near the base of the cabinet. Luxury margarine remains at spreading consistency and it's a good idea to keep a packet always in the refrigerator for easy-mix cakes (see page 167). In general, remove butter to be used in baking some time beforehand to allow it to soften for quicker mixing.

Eggs Do not wash eggs but store in the compartment provided. Before using in cooking, remove from the refrigerator and allow to warm up to room temperature. A better volume comes from egg whites if they are not chilled from the refrigerator. Egg whites at room temperature will absorb more air. Beat them in a cool corner of the kitchen, however, even on the back doorstep – the cooler the air incorporated the more the mixture rises in the oven.

Egg whites or egg yolks left over from cooking may be kept for one or two days. Collect whites in a covered container or jar, and keep yolks in a small cup or basin covered with water. Add yolks to sauces, custards or scrambled egg. Mark number of egg whites on outside of jar or container. If you forget, it doesn't matter – simply tip them out slowly from the jar. The albumen of egg white tends to cling together, and you can count them as they fall.

Fish Fish should be eaten as soon as possible; never keep fresh fish or shellfish for longer than 24 hours. Wipe or rinse under cold water and store unwrapped but covered with a sheet of waxed or cellophane paper. Oily fish, such as herrings, salmon or trout, keep fresh for a shorter time than white fish – any food containing a lot of fat keeps fresh for a shorter time. Cooked fish or shellfish will keep one or two days.

Fresh meat and poultry Always remove meat and poultry from the butcher's wrapping, that is unless it has been purchased in a supermarket where it is sealed in a vacuum pack. Raw meat should be lightly covered with waxed paper and put in the coldest part near the refrigerator unit or in the special meat tray.

Bacteria in meat attacks moist cut surfaces; for this reason a large joint will keep in perfect condition for up to five days and small cuts a slightly shorter time; on the other hand minced meat, which has many cut surfaces, no longer than 24 hours. See below:

Uncooked joints (beef, lamb or pork) – 5 days
Steak (frying or stewing) – 3 days
Minced meat – 1 day
Liver, kidneys or other offal – 1–2 days
Veal cutlets or chops – 3 days
Pork chops – 3 days

Chicken joints	– 2 days
Whole chicken unstuffed	– 3 days
(Prepared stuffing: place inside	
bird just before cooking)	– 2 days
Pork or beef sausages	– 3–4 days
Sliced, cooked, canned meat (opened)	– 2–3 days

Bacon Smoked or cured joints can be stored in the original wrapping if vacuum sealed, otherwise they should be wrapped in waxed paper or foil and placed on a low shelf. Bacon rashers will keep for one week.

Pastry Prepared puff, rough puff or flaky pastry wrapped in waxed paper or foil will keep for two days. Prepared shortcrust pastry will keep, too, but it is better to keep a rubbed-in short-crust pastry mixture to which water need only be added to make a pastry dough. A basic rubbed-in pastry mixture will keep for many weeks in a covered jar or polythene bag (see page 175).

Cheeses Hard cheese keeps perfectly for two or three weeks or more in a polythene bag, wrapped in aluminium foil or in a refrigerator box. Cheese spreads and cream cheese wrapped in foil keep up to a week and cottage cheese keeps three to five days. Very soft perishable cheeses keep 24 hours.

Whenever serving cheese simply on its own, remove it from the refrigerator at least an hour before serving, so it may come up to room temperature for the best flavour. Pieces of left-over cheese can be used to make potted cheeses or spreads. Grate small pieces of left-over Cheddar cheese, allow to dry and then store in a screw-topped jar.

Home-made potted meats, pâtés and spreads Keeping time may depend a little on the recipe but on the whole any cooked potted meat or pâté will keep up to one week and it should be stored either in the container in which it was cooked, or in a special pot, covered with a lid. Any cheese or meat spread for toast will also keep covered for up to a week (see page 27).

Casseroles cooked in advance and left-over cooked food Prepare any favourite casserole recipe, cool quickly and store in the refrigerator covered with a lid. Casseroles can be made one day in advance but no longer. Omit stirring in any last minute ingredients such as egg yolks or cream. When required, re-heat in a moderate oven (180°C, 355°F or Gas No. 4) for 30 minutes or until bubbling hot.

Sliced, cooked left-over meat should be covered with cling film wrapping, cooked soups poured into a basin and covered with a saucer; both keep one or two days. Always remove cooked stuffing from chicken or turkey carcass and store separately.

Vegetables and fruit Salad vegetables and citrus fruit benefit most from being stored in the refrigerator and keep three to five days. Vitamin C deteriorates rapidly at room temperature and when exposed to light. In this case, green vegetables such as spinach, cabbage and broccoli are better if washed, prepared and stored in a polythene bag in the refrigerator. All salad vegetables should be washed and placed in the vegetable crisper. Swing washed lettuce dry in a tea towel and store in a polythene bag in the refrigerator where it will crisp up nicely. Never toss salad in any dressing until ready to serve; the acid in the vinegar makes lettuce go limp.

Cut lemons or other fruit should be placed in a polythene bag, as much air as possible should be pressed out and the mouth of the bag closed with a twist tie.

Vegetables, except potatoes, can be prepared ahead for dinner parties and stored in polythene bags with the ends closed or in air-tight plastic food containers overnight.

Some fruits, such as melon, need only be chilled for an hour or so before serving. When cut, keep the slices closely covered to prevent the aroma from flavouring other foods. Bananas, however, dislike the cold and will quickly go black if stored in the refrigerator. Open canned or left-over cooked vegetables will keep up to three days – best to remove from the can.

Salad dressings and sauces During summer months it's a good idea to make up a large quantity of French dressing and store in the refrigerator in a screw-topped jar. Follow your favourite recipe and make 250 ml/½ pint at a time; it will keep up to two or three weeks – remember to shake well before using. Homemade mayonnaise will keep in covered plastic containers for one to two weeks, or it's a good idea to buy the sachets of fresh egg mayonnaise. Any fresh cream or soured cream dressing will keep up to three days.

Mineral water, fruit juices, syrups and wine It's inadvisable to take up valuable space storing these in the refrigerator. If, however, you plan on using them, tonic water and bitter lemon can be chilled and cans of tomato juice, fruit juices, beer, cider, or lager can be kept chilled. White wine to be served with a meal is nicest chilled for an hour or so beforehand.

Home-made fruit syrups for quick milk shakes are handy for children – they will keep for two or three weeks.

Ice cubes Keep ice trays always filled, individual plastic ice-cube moulds are handy for single ice cubes. For a large supply, keep extra cubes in a polythene bag in the frozen foods section. Either make cubes in rubber ice trays from which the cubes can be removed without dipping in cold water, or place the cubes on a tray and open freeze for five to ten minutes just to dry the outside surfaces. Then tip into a large bag for storage and they will not stick together. To make decorative ice cubes for summer drinks add maraschino cherries, pieces of lemon or orange, and make up cubes with mineral water which freezes clear, to show off the garnish.

Using the refrigerator

A wise cook doesn't simply use her refrigerator for storing perishable food but cooks and plans on using it to save time and money. Many recipes can be prepared ahead of time for baking later, left-over foods can be made into spreads for sandwiches. Pâtés and potted meats can provide instant meal starters or quick snacks, fruit syrups or home-made squashes provide drinks.

Shortcrust pastry, scone or cake ready-mixes It really depends on how often you plan on using these mixes as to whether it's worth making them or not. Small quantities of left-over stews or casseroles can be made into pies with extra meat from a can, or ready-made pie filling or bottled or canned fruits can fill fruit pies or flans, made with shortcrust. With extra sugar added, the mix can make a crumble topping for fresh or bottled fruit. See recipes for these, page 174.

Ready-made sauce mix A busy cook might find it an advantage to keep a basic roux at hand in the refrigerator. A cooked roux made from butter and flour is the basis of a white sauce. This can be prepared ahead in quantity and it can then be stored in a screw-topped jar. By stirring a little into hot milk, basic white sauce can be made very quickly. Prepare 200 g/8 oz of roux at a time (see recipes page 48) and store in the refrigerator. It will keep for up to one month.

Yeast dough mixes Yeast dough for breakfast rolls or tea breads can be prepared, covered and left overnight in the refrigerator for slow rising. Next day bring back to room temperature and bake according to recipe instructions.

Slice 'n' bake cookies

Slice 'n' bake cookie doughs are real time savers. The unbaked dough keeps for up to two weeks in the refrigerator. Wrap in foil or waxed paper ready for quick slicing and baking.

Honey cookies

Makes 24

100 g/4 oz plain flour	75 g/3 oz castor sugar
50 g/2 oz cornflour	1 rounded tablespoon honey
50 g/3 level teacups cornflakes	1 egg, lightly beaten
75 g/3 oz butter	50 g/2 oz ground almonds

Sift together the flour and cornflour on to a square of paper. Add the cornflakes and set aside. Cream the butter, sugar and honey until light. Beat in the egg and half the flour mixture. Turn on to a working surface, knead in rest of flour mixture and ground almonds. Shape into 6.5 mm/1½ in thick roll, wrap in foil; chill.

When ready to use, slice 5 mm/¼ in thick with a sharp knife and place on a greased baking tray. Place above centre in a moderately hot oven (190°C, 375°F or Gas No. 5) and bake for 10 minutes.

Walnut cookies
Makes 18–24

100 g/4 oz plain flour
1 level teaspoon baking powder
50 g/2 oz butter

25 g/1 oz castor sugar
1 tablespoon golden syrup
1 tablespoon coffee essence
50 g/2 oz finely chopped walnuts

Sift the flour and baking powder on to a square of paper and set aside. Cream the butter and sugar until light, then beat in the syrup and coffee essence. Add half the flour mixture and mix to a smooth paste, then add remaining flour and nuts and mix to a dough.

Turn the mixture out on to a lightly floured working surface. Divide the mixture in half and using lightly floured fingers shape each piece of dough into a fat roll about 15 mm/6 in long. Wrap in greaseproof paper or kitchen foil and twist the ends like a cracker. Place in the refrigerator until required to make cookies.

When ready to use, slice off with a sharp knife as many cookies as required in 5 m/¼ in thick slices and place on a greased baking tray. Replace remaining dough in the refrigerator and put sliced cookies in the centre of a moderate oven (180°C, 350°F or Gas No. 4) and bake for 15–20 minutes; they should be only very pale brown.

Savoury spreads and potted meats

Make these using a base of butter, which means they can be used to add extra flavour to sandwiches or to top grilled steaks or fish. Or cheese can be the base – useful for sandwiches or toppings for toast. Alternatively, they can be made with left-over or cooked meats or fresh meat and used for sandwiches, toast snacks or cocktail canapés.

Flavoured butters

Simply place all ingredients in a small basin and beat together. Cover basin with foil; alternatively, spoon into a small pot and cover with a lid. Keeps up to a week at a time in the refrigerator.

Anchovy Cream together 50 g/2 oz butter, 1 level teaspoon anchovy essence, salt and pepper to taste. Use in sandwiches with tomato, bacon or cold meat or use to top grilled fish.

Parsley Cream together 50 g/2 oz butter or margarine, 1 rounded teaspoon chopped parsley, salt, pepper and squeeze of lemon juice.

Use in sandwiches with cheese, eggs, canned salmon or crab or to top grilled chicken joints, steaks, Dover sole or fish cutlets.

Cheese and chutney Cream together 50 g/2 oz butter, 25 g/1 oz grated cheese, 1 level tablespoon chutney (chop up any large pieces), salt and pepper to taste. Use in sandwiches with sliced tomato or ham or use to top grilled fish cutlets.

Mustard Cream together 50 g/2 oz butter, 1 rounded teaspoon prepared English mustard and squeeze of lemon juice.

Use in sandwiches with ham or cheese or cold beef or use to top grilled steaks or chicken joints.

Potted cheese

Makes enough for about 24 biscuits

100 g/4 oz English Cheddar
50 g/2 oz soft butter
freshly milled pepper

pinch ground mace
2 tablespoons medium dry sherry

Pound the finely grated cheese with the butter, pepper and mace. Add the sherry and mix thoroughly. Spoon into a small pot, cover and store in the refrigerator. Use as required, spread on biscuits or for cocktail canapés.

Chicken liver and bacon spread

400 g/1 lb chicken livers
50 g/2 oz butter or margarine
½ small onion, finely chopped
3 rashers streaky bacon, trimmed
  and chopped

1 level teaspoon salt
freshly milled black pepper
¼ level teaspoon ground nutmeg
3 tablespoons mayonnaise

Wash the livers well in cold, salted water and drain; using scissors trim away any skin. Add to the hot butter in a medium saucepan, along with the onion and bacon. Fry quickly at first, till livers are browned, and then lower heat and cook gently, covered with a lid for 5 minutes. Draw pan off heat and pass this mixture through the fine blade of a mincer into a medium-sized basin. Add the seasoning, nutmeg, and mayonnaise, stirring well to blend. Pour into a 1 pint pâté or china dish and set in a cool place until mixture is quite firm. Use as a filling for sandwiches, or spread on biscuits for canapés or hot toast.

Hungarian cheese spread

Makes enough for 12 sandwiches
100 g/4 oz cream cheese
50 g/2 oz butter
1 teaspoon anchovy paste
1 teaspoon made mustard

2 level teaspoons paprika pepper
2 teaspoons chopped capers
6 grinds of black pepper
2 teaspoons chopped chives

Cream the butter until soft and then add the cream cheese and beat well. Then beat in the anchovy paste, mustard, paprika, chopped capers, seasoning and chopped chives. The mixture will be a beautiful salmon pink. Spoon into an earthenware serving pot and refrigerate. Nice for a sandwich filling with crisp lettuce, as a spread on cheese biscuits or crusty bread – no butter required.

Potted turkey or chicken

Makes enough for 12 sandwiches or toast slices

2–3 bacon rashers
200–250 g/8–10 oz cooked turkey
  or chicken meat sliced
pinch ground mace

dash Worcestershire sauce
50–75 g/2–3 oz butter
salt and pepper

Fry the trimmed bacon rashers until quite crisp. Pass these through the fine blade of the mincer along with the chicken or turkey meat into a mixing basin. Add a pinch of ground mace, Worcestershire sauce and beat in the butter. Taste and season with salt and pepper if necessary.

Pack into a small pot and cover with extra melted butter or a lid and store in a refrigerator. Use as a spread on toast or in sandwiches.

Smoked cod's roe pâté

Serves 6

200 g/8 oz smoked cod's roe
2 small slices white bread, crusts
  removed
2 tablespoons milk
6 tablespoons oil

2 tablespoons lemon juice
salt and pepper
1 teaspoon finely chopped parsley

Scoop the cod's roe out of the skin using a teaspoon and pound in a mortar with a pestle or beat with a wooden spoon until smooth. Soak the bread in the milk, then squeeze out as much milk as possible. Add the bread to the smoked roe and mix the two together thoroughly. Using a wooden spoon, beat in the oil one tablespoon at a time alternating it with the lemon juice. Add seasoning of salt and pepper and the chopped parsley. Spoon into small pot, cover and keep in refrigerator. Keeps up to 1 week. Nice as a sandwich filling with crisp lettuce, or served with hot toast for a starter.

Chicken liver pâté

Serves 4

200 g/8 oz chicken livers	grated nutmeg
100 g/4 oz butter	bay leaf and melted butter for the
1 teaspoon brandy or sherry	top
salt and freshly milled pepper	

Trim the chicken livers and set aside. Melt half the butter in a saucepan, add the livers and fry gently covered with a lid for 5 minutes. Draw off the heat and pass the livers and juice from the pan through a food mill or blend to a puré in an electric blender. Add the brandy or sherry. Cream the remaining butter in a mixing basin, add the liver mixture and beat thoroughly. Season with salt and pepper and a little grated nutmeg. Press the mixture into a serving dish. Run a little melted butter over the surface, garnish with a bay leaf and chill. Store in the refrigerator. Keeps 1 week. Nice with hot toast for a starter or spread on canapé biscuits.

Concentrated fruit syrups and cordials

Kept chilled in the refrigerator, these make marvellous summer drinks in hot weather. Label the bottles and the quantity required to make up a drink.

Lemon cordial

Fills 2 quart lemonade bottles
2 large juicy lemons
600 g/1½ lb granulated sugar
25 g/1 oz citric or tartaric acid
2 pints/1 litre water

Scrub the lemons and then pare the rind thinly with a vegetable parer. Place the lemon rinds, granulated sugar and citric or tartaric acid in a good-sized mixing basin. Measure the water into a saucepan and bring to the boil. Pour over the ingredients and stir to dissolve the sugar. Leave until quite cold. Strain the mixture to get rid of the lemon peel and add the juice from the two used lemons. Pour into bottles – this amount almost exactly fills two large lemonade bottles. To use: fill a tumbler one third full with the syrup and top up with water. Or you can make a long drink by including ice and lemon slices and using soda water instead.

Lemon ginger syrup

Makes 1¼/2½ pints

50 g/2 oz root ginger
1 litre/2 pints water
thinly peeled rind of 1 lemon

800 g/2 lb granulated sugar
juice of 2 lemons

Bruise the root ginger with a rolling pin or heavy weight and then place in a medium-sized heavy saucepan. Pour in the water and add the lemon peel. Bring to the boil and simmer gently covered with a lid for 45 minutes. Draw the pan off the heat and make up the liquid to 1 litre/2 pints. Strain and then return to the pan with the sugar and stir slowly over a low heat until the sugar has dissolved, then draw the pan off the heat and stir in the strained lemon juice. Pour the syrup into the bottles and cover.

This syrup will keep for several weeks in a refrigerator. To use the syrup – fill a tumbler one third full with the syrup and fill up with hot or iced water. Decorate with a slice of lemon.

Frozen foods

Unless for immediate consumption within 24 hours, frozen foods should be stored in the frozen food compartment of a refrigerator. Accurate storage of frozen foods depends on the temperature of the compartment – in other words, the lower the temperature the longer the food will keep. There is now a new method of guidance for the home cook which consists of star marking on both frozen foods and the frozen food compartment.

If your refrigerator has one star, it means the frozen food compartment operates at under −6°C/21°F and will keep frozen foods for one week. With two stars, the frozen food compartment operates below −12°C/10°F, and the frozen foods will keep for a month. Three stars and a temperature not higher than $-18°C/0°F$, means that the foods will keep for three months.

A good frozen food compartment in your refrigerator gives plenty of scope for stocking up with quick frozen foods. Select the ones you buy carefully and *plan on using them*.

Quick soups

Although, on the whole, soup making involves lengthy preparation, there are many short cuts. Starchy vegetables, such as potatoes or carrots, cook more quickly when finely grated, and can form the basis of vegetable soups. Stock cubes can be used for clear broth with added vegetables and as a flavouring stock in other soups.

To make any soup your own speciality in an instant, dress it up with a garnish or serve with hot breads. Soups lend themselves to a variety of garnishes – anything from a sprinkling of chopped parsley to shredded cheese. Parmesan croûtons are a delicious accompaniment.

Sprinkle crumbled fried bacon pieces, grated cheese, paprika pepper, chopped parsley or toast slices cut in tiny dice, over tomato, asparagus, celery, mushroom or any vegetable soup.

Stir chopped chives, fresh cream, diced hard-boiled eggs, chopped green pepper or snipped watercress leaves into any cream soup. Chives are specially tasty in potato soup.

Cut thin slices of lemon or cucumber and float on top of consommé, beef or chicken bouillon or oxtail soup.

Add sliced frankfurter sausages or shredded cheese over heartier soups such as bean and bacon, scotch broth, lentil, vegetable or chicken and rice.

Parmesan croûtons

Serves 4

3 slices of white bread, crusts
  removed
25 g/1 oz butter

1 heaped tablespoon grated
  Parmesan cheese

Cut the bread into 5 mm/¼ in cubes and sauté in the hot butter until golden brown. Add the cheese, tossing to mix well then serve hot.

Melba toast

Serves 4

6 slices white bread, crusts
  removed

First toast the bread slices on both sides until golden brown. Cut off the crusts and then carefully split each one into two thin slices. Cut each new slice diagonally to make triangles and toast again, the inside this time. Store in an air-tight tin.

Seeded bread slices

Serves 4

4–6 slices French bread
butter for spreading
poppy, caraway or sesame seeds

Sprinkle buttered bread slices with caraway, poppy or sesame seeds. Heat in a moderate oven (180°C, 350°F or Gas No. 4) or toast under a hot grill.

Re-heating bread and rolls All types of rolls served with soup are very much nicer if served hot. First wrap in foil and place in a moderately hot oven (190°C, 375°F or Gas No. 5) for 15 minutes. Protected by foil, they re-heat without becoming dry and are in no danger of burning if forgotten for a while!

Clear vegetable soup

Serves 6–8

750 ml/1½ pints water
2 beef stock cubes
2 tablespoons dry sherry

2–3 tablespoons cooked diced
   vegetables or 1 small packet
   frozen mixed vegetables

Measure the water into a saucepan and bring almost to the boil. Crumble in the stock cubes and stir until dissolved. Add the sherry and cooked vegetables and heat through before serving, or add the frozen vegetables and simmer for a further 5 minutes.

Quick potato soup

Serves 6–8

750 ml/1½ pints water
2 chicken or beef stock cubes
40 g/1 lb potatoes
1 large onion
125 ml/¼ pint milk

50 g/2 oz butter
salt and pepper
chopped parsley and grated
   cheese for garnish

Measure the water into a saucepan and bring up to the boil. Crumble in the stock cubes and stir until dissolved. Peel both potatoes and onion and grate coarsely. Add to the stock and simmer until tender and potatoes are quite soft – takes about 15 minutes. Pass the soup through a sieve or blender and return to the saucepan. Add the milk and butter, check seasoning, and re-heat. Serve sprinkled with parsley and cheese.

Clear mushroom consommé

Serves 4–6

40 g/1½ oz butter
1 large onion, finely chopped
100 g/4 oz mushrooms, thickly
   sliced

1 litre/2 pints stock
juice of ½ lemon
seasoning
2 tablespoons sherry

Melt the butter in a saucepan and gently fry the onion until tender and lightly browned. Add the mushrooms and fry a further 5 minutes. Add the stock and lemon juice and bring just up to the boil. Draw the pan off the heat, check seasoning, stir in the sherry and serve. This consommé makes a very suitable first course for a dinner party.

Quick cream of chicken soup

Serves 4–6

625 ml/1¼ pints water
2 chicken stock cubes
1 egg yolk
125 ml/¼ pint single cream

salt and pepper
dash nutmeg
chopped parsley for garnish

Measure the water into a saucepan and bring up to the boil. Crumble in the chicken stock cubes and stir until dissolved. Blend the egg yolk with the cream and stir into the soup. Reheat but do not allow to boil. Draw the pan off the heat, check seasoning and add a dash of nutmeg. Sprinkle with parsley and serve.

Courgette soup

Serves 4

25 g/1 oz butter
1 large onion, finely chopped
400 g/1lb courgettes

750 ml/1½ pints water
2 chicken stock cubes
salt and freshly milled pepper

Melt the butter in a large saucepan. Add the onion and sauté gently for about 5 minutes or until the onion is soft but not brown. Trim and slice the courgettes (no need to peel), add to the pan and mix with the butter and onion. Stir in the water, add the chicken stock cubes and bring to a simmer. Cover and cook gently for 30 minutes. Draw off the heat and blend the liquid and vegetables in a blender. Return the soup to the pan, season with salt and pepper, reheat and serve.

Prawn chowder

Serves 4

25 g/1 oz butter
1 onion, finely chopped
500 ml/1 pint water
1 chicken stock cube
3 medium potatoes, cut in dice
salt and freshly milled pepper
250 ml/½ pint milk

1 teaspoon concentrated tomato
 purée
1 (225 g/8 oz) packet frozen
 prawns
salt and freshly milled pepper
25–50 g/1–2 oz grated cheese

Heat the butter in a saucepan and add the onion. Cook gently to soften the onion, then add the potato and toss in the onion and butter. Stir in the water and stock cube and bring to a simmer. Cook gently for 15 minutes or until potato has softened and draw off the heat. Pass liquid and vegetables through an electric blender to purée and return to the saucepan.

Stir in the milk. Add the tomato purée, a seasoning of salt and pepper and the prawns. Reheat gently to thaw prawns and reheat soup. Stir in grated cheese and serve in soup bowls.

Avocado soup

Serves 4–6

2 ripe avocados
750 ml/1½ pints water
2 chicken stock cubes
125 ml/¼ pint single cream

juice ½ lemon
salt and freshly milled pepper
chopped chives

Halve the avocados and remove the stones. Scoop out the flesh into the glass container of an electric blender. Make the stock with the chicken stock cubes and water, and add half the stock to the blender. Cover and blend for a few moments until soup is smooth. Pour into a bowl, add rest of stock and stir in the cream, lemon juice and a seasoning of salt and pepper to taste. Chill well. Stir in chopped chives before serving.

Tomato and onion soup

Serves 4–6

25 g/1 oz butter
2 onions, peeled and sliced
1 × 400 g/14 oz can peeled
  tomatoes
1 level teaspoon sugar
salt and pepper

1 level tablespoon flour
1 teaspoon Worcestershire sauce
375 ml/¾ pint stock or water
  plus stock cube
125 ml/¼ pint single cream or
  top of the milk

Heat the butter in a saucepan and add the onions. Cover with a lid and fry gently until onions are soft – about 5 minutes. Spoon into the blender with the contents of the can of tomatoes, sugar, salt and pepper, flour, Worcestershire sauce and stock. Blend on high speed for 1 minute. Then return the soup to the saucepan. Bring the soup up to the boil, stirring all the time until thickened and boiling.

Draw the pan off the heat, stir in the cream, check seasoning and serve.

Chilled summer soup

Serves 9

2 × 298 g/10½ oz cans
  condensed tomato soup
1½ soup cans water

1 × 142 ml/5 fl oz carton soured
  cream
chopped parsley or chives for
  garnish

Combine the soup, water and soured cream. Beat with a rotary beater until smooth then chill for several hours. Serve in chilled soup bowls, sprinkled with parsley or chives.

Broccoli soup

Serves 4

1 × 225g/8 oz packet frozen
  broccoli
250 ml/½ pint stock or use water
plus beef stock cube
1 small onion, peeled and halved

pinch pepper and nutmeg
pinch salt
125 ml/¼ pint single cream
chopped chives or parsley for
  garnish

Place broccoli in a saucepan together with the stock, bring to the boil, cover with a lid and simmer gently until tender – takes about 10–15 minutes.

Draw pan off the heat, add the onion and pour into the glass container of the food blender. Blend until broccoli is a purée; return to the saucepan. Stir in seasoning and cream and re-heat but do not boil. Serve topped with chives or parsley.

To serve chilled: Pour blended soup into a mixing basin. Stir in seasoning and cream and chill until ready to serve. Pour into chilled soup bowls and serve sprinkled with chives or parsley.

Cream of mushroom soup

Serves 4–5

200 g/ 8 oz mushrooms, trimmed
  and sliced
1 small onion, peeled and sliced
1 oz butter
375 ml/¾ pint stock or water plus
  stock cube

125 ml/¼ pint milk
2 level tablespoons cornflour
1 level teaspoon salt
pinch pepper

Add the mushrooms and onion to the hot butter in a frying pan.

Fry gently for 2–3 minutes to soften the onion then spoon into the electric blender and add the stock, milk, cornflour and seasonings. Blend on high speed for 1 minute, then pour the soup back into the saucepan. Stir over moderate heat until soup thickens and comes up to the boil. Draw the pan off the heat, check seasoning and serve.

Sweet corn soup

Serves 6

2 × 354 g/12 oz tins sweet corn
375 ml/¾ pint water
1 chicken stock cube
25 g/1 oz butter
1 small onion, finely chopped

1 level tablespoon flour
500 ml/1 pint milk
1 level teaspoon salt
2–3 tablespoons single cream
chopped parsley to garnish

Drain liquid from the tins of sweet corn and empty the corn into a saucepan. Add the water and stock cube and simmer gently for about 15 minutes or until the corn is tender. Draw off the heat and pass corn and stock through an electric blender to make a purée.

Melt the butter in the clean saucepan over low heat. Add the chopped onion and cook gently for about 5 minutes or until onion is soft but not brown. Stir in the flour, then gradually add the milk stirring well all the time to get a thin sauce. Add the sweet corn purée and bring to a simmer. Cook 2–3 minutes, then draw off the heat and stir in the cream. Sprinkle with chopped parsley for serving.

Curried chicken soup

Serves 4

1 × 298 g/10½ oz can condensed
  cream of chicken soup
1 soup can milk

½ level teaspoon curry powder
2 tablespoons chopped parsley for
  garnish

Pour the soup, milk and curry powder into a mixing basin and blend until smooth. Chill in a refrigerator until ready to serve.

Pour into chilled soup bowls and sprinkle the tops with parsley.

Canned soups

Canned soups have tremendous advantages for a busy cook and since they store well, it is a good plan to have a wide selection always in stock. Soups of different flavours can be combined together or, to basic cream or condensed soups, extra vegetables may be added. For instance, a small can of creamed style sweet corn may be stirred into tomato soup, a can of drained, cut asparagus spears can make cream or condensed asparagus soup look home-made, or to chicken soup add thawed frozen peas or heat up beef consommé with a tablespoon of sherry and serve with a garnish of thinly sliced lemon or chopped parsley.

In summer, or for any special occasion, fresh iced soups make a pleasant change. Serve them really cold in chilled soup bowls. For simple quick recipes, cream of asparagus, celery, chicken, mushroom or tomato soup all made with milk and chilled are delicious. Beef consommé can be chilled in the can or poured into a bowl with 1 tablespoon of sherry added and chilled. Serve any of the soups topped with chopped parsley or chives.

When preparing condensed soups, empty the can into a bowl or saucepan and stir to make it smooth. Then gradually add the water or milk, stirring in a little at a time and blend well before continuing with the recipe.

Soups from left-overs

Mulligatawny soup Can be made using left-over curry sauce and a little boiled rice. Mix together 150 ml/1 teacupful curry sauce with 500 ml/1 pint stock (use water and stock cube) blended with 25 g/1 oz flour. Stir till boiling. Check seasoning and consistency. Stir in 1–2 tablespoons boiled rice and a few meat or chicken scraps if available. You could make this same soup if you have some left-over chicken or meat curry.

Spinach soup Can be made using cooked spinach. Put 150 ml/1 teacupful chopped, cooked spinach into a pan with 25 g/1 oz butter and reheat gently. Stir in 500 ml/1 pint thin white sauce – made using 500 ml/1 pint milk infused with an onion and stirred into a blend of 25 g/1 oz butter and 2 level tablespoons flour. Reheat sauce and spinach until boiling, then purée. Thin down with milk or stock and reheat. Check seasoning and serve.

Mixed vegetable soup Heat up 200–300 g/8–12 oz cooked mixed vegetables – carrots, leeks, onions, cauliflower or potato in 500 ml/1 pint thin white sauce. Rub through a sieve and reheat. Thin down with stock if necessary. Reheat and sprinkle with chopped parsley. Even quicker vegetable soups can be made by puréeing left-over cooked vegetables in a white sauce – onions or cauliflower in white sauce for example – with a stock in the blender. Then reheat and serve.

Minute savers

*To make any cream or concentrated soup go further, add a chicken stock cube and a whole extra can of water.

*When heating canned soups, bring only just up to the boil. Stir constantly too – over-boiling or scorching will spoil the flavour.

*When using concentrated soups, empty the contents of the soup can into the saucepan first. Then with a wooden spoon slowly stir the liquid and blend well before placing over the heat.

*To make a very quick jellied consommé – make a beef or chicken stock cube up to 375 ml/¾ pint with 1 level tablespoon aspic jelly crystals; add 1 tablespoon dry sherry and leave to cool. Stir with a fork when almost setting.

*If you haven't got a measure for liquids, remember that a teacup holds 150 ml/⅓ pint and a tumbler holds 250 ml/½ pint. Even use a clean milk bottle 500 ml/1 pint to measure the water for soups.

*When blending soups in a liquidizer always ladle in a little of the vegetables and some of the liquid each time for a smoother purée.

Speedy sauces

A basic white sauce is in itself quite simple and quick to make. For added speed and ease, either use a blending method where the milk and flour are whisked together before adding to the melted butter or make the roux mix of flour and butter beforehand and store ready for use.

Easy basic white sauce

Makes 250 ml/½ pint
25 g/1 oz butter or margarine
250 ml/½ pint milk
25 g/1 oz plain flour
salt and pepper

Place the butter or margarine in a saucepan and set over low heat to melt. Meanwhile measure the cold milk into a medium-sized mixing basin and sift the flour on to it. Using a whisk or rotary hand beater, mix the two quickly and thoroughly together.

Pour the blend into the melted fat and cook, stirrring all the time until the mixture has thickened and is boiling. Cook the mixture for 2–3 minutes, then season well with salt and pepper and use as required.

This method makes a medium-thick pouring sauce; if a thinner sauce is required, add a little extra milk. For a thicker sauce, use a little less milk than the recipe states. Always remember it's easier to add extra milk afterwards.

Checking errors

However carefully recipes are followed, there's always the possibility that something can go wrong and often in the case of sauces the consistency is not quite as expected.

If your sauce is too thin Mix flour and cold water to form a smooth paste, using 1 level tablespoon flour to 1½ tablespoons cold water. Add gradually to the sauce, stirring until thickened.

If your sauce is too thick Stir or beat in a little more of the liquid used in the sauce – in this case, milk. Remember to re-check seasonings.

If your sauce is lumpy Beat thoroughly with a rotary hand beater or electric whisk and then strain into a second saucepan. Or blend for a few seconds in an electric liquidizer if you're fortunate enough to have one.

If your sauce has to stand Don't stir in all the liquid stated in the recipe – leave 2–3 tablespoons. Allow the sauce to thicken, then add the remaining liquid but do not stir in. Allow this liquid to remain on the surface of the sauce and it will prevent a skin forming. When ready to serve, stir in the liquid and use the sauce. Never leave a sauce standing over even the lowest heat for any length of time – it will eventually scorch. Take a chef's tip and set the base of the pan in a larger roasting tin of simmering water – this way it will keep hot but not burn.

Variations of the basic white sauce
There are many variations of any basic sauce; always remember to cook the sauce and season to taste before adding any of the extra ingredients.

Cheese sauce Add 50 g/2 oz grated Cheddar cheese and ¼ teaspoon made mustard, after the sauce has cooked. Stir until cheese has melted. Serve over fish, eggs, macaroni or vegetables.
  Note: If the sauce is to be used as a base for macaroni and cheese, increase cheese in sauce to 75 g/3 oz.

Hard-boiled egg sauce Coarsely chop 1 hard-boiled egg and add to the sauce after it has cooked. Do not stir the sauce more than necessary, otherwise the egg will break up too much and spoil the appearance. Serve with fish or vegetable dishes.

Caper sauce Add about 2 teaspoons of chopped capers and a squeeze of lemon juice to the sauce after the sauce has cooked. Serve over boiled mutton or veal.

Parsley sauce Add 1 tablespoon finely chopped parsley to the cooked sauce. Remember to wash the parsley before chopping, then squeeze dry in the corner of a cloth to prevent the parsley from discolouring the sauce. Serve over fish dishes, baked ham or broad beans.

Shrimp sauce Add a few picked shrimps or a small carton of potted shrimps to the cooked sauce. Add a little anchovy essence for extra flavour or a tablespoon tomato ketchup if a pink sauce is required. Serve over fish dishes.

Mustard sauce Add 2 level teaspoons mustard powder blended smoothly with 1 tablespoon vinegar to the cooked sauce. Serve over herring, mackerel, cauliflower or boiled meats.

Canned tomato sauce

Serves 4

1 onion, peeled and finely chopped	1 level tablespoon castor sugar
15 g/½ oz butter	½ level teaspoon dried mixed herbs
1 × 400 g/14 oz can tomatoes	salt and freshly milled pepper
water – see recipe	
2 level tablespoons cornflour	

Add the onion to the melted butter in the saucepan. Cook gently for 2–3 minutes to soften the onion but do not allow to brown. Add the contents of the can of tomatoes and half the can of water blended with the cornflour, sugar (tomatoes always taste better with a little sweetness), herbs and a seasoning of salt and pepper. Stir until the mixture is boiling and thickened, then simmer gently for 5 minutes. Draw the pan off the heat, and pass the sauce through a sieve. Check seasoning and serve.

Fresh tomato sauce

Serves 4

600 g/1½ lb fresh tomatoes
1 large onion, peeled and thinly
  sliced
1 clove garlic, crushed with salt
¼ teaspoon dried thyme
1 bay leaf
15 g/½ oz butter
2 level tablespoons plain flour
1 level teaspoon salt
freshly milled pepper

Nick the skins on the tomatoes and plunge into boiling water for 1 minute. Drain and peel off the skins. Halve the tomatoes and place in a saucepan along with the onion, finely chopped garlic, thyme and the bay leaf. Simmer for about 15–20 minutes, covered with a lid. Squash the tomatoes with a wooden spoon occasionally until quite tender and soft. Pass the tomatoes through a sieve or pass through a mincer and return the purée to the saucepan. Cream the butter and flour to make a paste and add to the tomato purée. Stir over moderate heat until the sauce has thickened and is boiling. Add the salt and a seasoning of pepper and simmer for 2–3 minutes.

Wine and onion sauce

Serves 4

50 g/2 oz butter or margarine
1 large onion, peeled and finely
  chopped
150 ml/⅓ pint dry white wine
2 tablespoons wine vinegar
1 level teaspoon sugar
1 level teaspoon salt
freshly milled pepper
50 g/2 oz butter
1 level tablespoon plain flour

Melt the butter in a medium-sized saucepan, add the onion, and cook gently for 5 minutes. Stir in the white wine, vinegar, sugar, and salt and pepper to taste, and bring to the boil; reduce heat and simmer gently for 5 minutes.

Draw the pan off the heat and add the creamed butter and flour in small pieces. Stir to blend thoroughly, then return to the heat, and still stirring all the time, bring up to the boil. Simmer for 1–2 minutes. Serve sauce over grilled or fried steak.

Quick barbecue sauce

Serves 4

2 tablespoons salad oil
1 onion, finely chopped
150 ml/¹/₃ pint tomato ketchup
4 tablespoons vinegar
50 g/2 oz soft brown sugar

2 rounded teaspoons made
  mustard
2 tablespoons Worcestershire
  sauce
½ level teaspoon salt

Heat the oil in a small saucepan, add the onion and fry gently for 5 minutes until tender. Add all the remaining ingredients; bring slowly up to the boil and allow to simmer for 10 minutes.

Pineapple sweet and sour sauce

Serves 4–6

1 × 340 g/12 oz can pineapple
  chunks
4 tablespoons vinegar
75 g/3 oz soft brown sugar

1 tablespoon soy sauce
¼ level teaspoon salt
2 level tablespoons cornflour

Drain the pineapple from the can and reserve the syrup, making it up to 250 ml/½ pint with water. Combine this with the vinegar, brown sugar, soy sauce and salt. Measure the cornflour into a medium-sized saucepan and moisten with a little of the liquid, mixing to a smooth paste. Stir in the remaining liquid and cook over moderate heat until thickened and boiling. Add pineapple chunks and draw pan off the heat. Serve with pork chops or grilled gammon rashers.

Fresh mushroom sauce

Serves 4

25 g/1 oz butter
100 g/4 oz button mushrooms
salt and pepper
pinch mixed herbs

1 level tablespoon flour
125 ml/¼ pint creamy milk
1 tablespoon chopped parsley

Melt the butter in a frying pan over moderate heat and add the prepared mushrooms. Button mushrooms are the small closed mushrooms; they are the best kind to use in a sauce because they look nicer and they don't discolour the sauce as much as the very

open black ones. Cultivated mushrooms do not need peeling:
rinse under cold water, trim stalks, pat dry and slice.

Fry the mushrooms fairly quickly for about 1 minute, tossing
them to cook evenly. Add a good seasoning of salt and freshly
milled pepper, herbs and the flour. Stir to blend and then gradually stir in the milk and bring up to the boil, stirring all the time
until thickened. Allow to simmer gently for 1–2 minutes, add
parsley and draw off heat. If over-cooked, mushroom sauce will
discolour very quickly due to the dark juices being drawn out of
mushrooms. Serve with steak, liver, chicken or kidneys.

Quick sauces using a ready-made roux

If you're a cook that uses sauces a good deal it might be an
advantage to make the roux, that is the cooked butter and flour
basis for any sauce, in a quantity and store it in the refrigerator
ready made. This is particularly time saving for brown sauces
where the roux may take up to 40 minutes to colour properly.

It's best to make one mix to be used for white sauce – it's
important that this roux does not brown, otherwise the resulting
sauce would be discoloured – and a second mix for brown sauce
– this roux in fact has to be cooked until quite dark in colour.

To make a roux mix for white sauces Melt 200 g/8 oz butter or
margarine in a heavy saucepan and stir in 200 g/8 oz plain flour.
Cook over low heat, stirring occasionally to prevent the mix from
sticking to the pan base and browning. As the roux cooks it will
become lighter in colour and slightly sandy or crumbly in texture.
When ready – takes about 15 minutes – draw the pan off the heat
and allow to stand until cool, stirring occasionally. Then spoon
into a screw-topped jar – a small Kilner jar is good – cover and
store in the refrigerator.

To use the roux for white sauces Heat 250 ml/½ pint milk in a
saucepan until almost boiling. Then draw the pan off the heat
and add 2 tablespoons of the roux mix. Stir until the roux has
melted then replace over moderate heat and stir until the sauce
thickens and is boiling. Cook gently for 2–3 minutes then season

well and use as required. Any of the variations given for basic white sauce may be used with this sauce.

To make a roux mix for brown sauces Melt 200 g/8 oz white cooking fat or dripping in a heavy saucepan and stir in 300 g/12 oz plain flour. This time cook gently stirring occasionally but allow the roux to brown gently and evenly. Eventually the mixture should be quite dark brown in colour, but take care not to allow it to burn. When ready – takes about 40 minutes – draw the pan off the heat and allow to cool, stirring occasionally. Then spoon into a screw-topped jar, cover and store in the refrigerator.

To use the roux for brown sauces Heat 375 ml/¾ pint water in a saucepan until almost boiling, then crumble in a beef or chicken stock cube and stir until dissolved. Draw the pan off the heat and add 3 tablespoons of brown roux mix. Stir until roux has melted, then replace the pan over moderate heat and stir until sauce has thickened and boiled. Cook for 2–3 minutes then season well with salt and pepper and use as required.

Variations of the basic brown sauce
Espagnole sauce Follow the recipe above, using only 250 ml/½ pint water and 1 × 400 g/14 oz can tomatoes. Add a few bacon rinds and chopped mushrooms for flavour and simmer an extra 10 minutes. Strain the sauce before using.

Use the sauce in basic stews or casseroles, or serve with fried liver or meat or for re-heating cold slices of beef or lamb.

Piquante sauce Into the basic brown sauce, stir 1 teaspoon made mustard, 1 tablespoon redcurrant jelly, ½ level teaspoon paprika (not the hot cayenne pepper) and 1 tablespoon vinegar. Simmer to dissolve the jelly and blend flavourings.

Serve with sausages and hamburgers.

Curry sauce Prepare the basic brown sauce and, while simmering, in a separate saucepan melt 15 g/½ oz butter; add peeled and finely chopped onion. Cover with a lid and fry gently to soften the onion, stir in 2 level tablespoons curry powder, or more for a hot curry, and fry gently for a further 5 minutes. Then stir in the cooked brown sauce, 1 tablespoon chutney – chop up any large pieces – and a squeeze of lemon juice. Bring up to the boil and serve.

Excellent with cooked meat or quartered hard-boiled eggs. Or pour over fresh cubed steak or chicken joints and casserole in the oven following a normal curry recipe.

Mushroom sauce Prepare the basic brown sauce and, while simmering, in a separate pan fry 100 g/4 oz trimmed sliced mushrooms in 25 g/1 oz butter. Stir in the cooked sauce, re-heat and serve with sausages, hamburgers, liver or steak.

Quick sauces for meat, poultry, vegetables and fish

Make all sorts of quick sauces using ketchups, table sauces, pickles and chutneys or herbs, seasonings and spices for extra flavouring.

Quick cheese sauce

Serves 6
1 × 298 g/10½ oz can condensed
  cream of celery or chicken soup
125 ml/¼ pint milk
100 g/4 oz grated Cheddar cheese

In a saucepan combine together the soup and milk, stirring to blend. Add the cheese and stir over low heat until cheese is melted and sauce is hot. Serve over fish, omelette or vegetables.

Stroganoff sauce

Serves 2–3

1 small onion
25 g/1 oz butter
50 g/2 oz button mushrooms

½ teaspoon tomato purée
142 ml/5 fl oz carton soured cream
salt and freshly ground pepper

Peel and finely chop the onion. Melt the butter in a frying pan, add the onion and fry gently for a few minutes to soften. Trim and slice the mushrooms, add to the pan and cook gently for about 15 minutes.

Stir in the tomato purée and soured cream and bring just up to the boil. Season to taste with salt and pepper and serve hot with grilled steak or chicken.

Jiffy barbecue sauce

Serves 4
125 ml/¼ pint tomato ketchup
1 rounded teaspoon dry mustard
dash Tabasco sauce
1 tablespoon Worcestershire sauce

Combine all ingredients together in a saucepan and heat until almost boiling. Serve over frankfurters, hamburgers, or steaks or chicken joints.

Chutney sauce

Serves 4
3 heaped tablespoons mango
  chutney
75 g/3 oz castor sugar

3 tablespoons water
juice of 1 lemon

Measure the chutney into a saucepan, chopping up any large pieces. Add the sugar, water and strained lemon juice. Stir over low heat to dissolve the sugar then bring up to the boil. Simmer quickly for 1–2 minutes until slightly thickened then draw the pan off the heat.

Serve with gammon, tongue, grilled sausages, or pork chops.

Caper sauce

Serves 4
50 g/2 oz butter
juice ½ lemon
1 tablespoon capers
1 tablespoon chopped parsley

Melt the butter in a saucepan over low heat, add the strained lemon juice, capers and parsley and stir to blend.

Serve with roast lamb, grilled steak, fish or fresh cooked asparagus.

Spiced cranberry sauce

Serves 4

1 × 184 g/6½ oz jar cranberry
  sauce
1 tablespoon vinegar or dry
  sherry

¼ teaspoon made mustard
pinch ground cinnamon and
  ground cloves

Empty the contents of the cranberry sauce into a saucepan. Add
the vinegar or sherry, mustard and spices. Stir over low heat
until jelly melts. Serve with baked boiled bacon, or grilled pork
chops.

Sour cream horseradish sauce

Serves 4–6

4 tablespoons prepared
  horseradish relish
1 × 142 ml/5 fl oz carton soured
  cream

salt and freshly ground pepper
dash of Worcestershire sauce

In a basin mix together the horseradish relish and soured cream.
Add a seasoning of salt and pepper and a dash of Worcestershire
sauce. Allow to stand for 1 hour before serving.
  Serve with hot or cold roast beef, and grilled steaks.

Steak sauce

Serves 4

50 g/2 oz butter
2 tablespoons tomato ketchup
1½ teaspoons Worcestershire
  sauce

1 teaspoon made mustard
juice of ½ lemon

Melt the butter in a small saucepan, then stir in the ketchup,
Worcestershire sauce, mustard and strained lemon juice. Heat
through gently but do not allow to boil. Serve with grilled or
fried steak, chops, hamburgers or sausages.

Just for vegetables

Parsley cream sauce

Serves 4

125 ml/¼ pint double cream
squeeze of lemon juice
salt and freshly milled pepper

1 teaspoon finely chopped parsley
  or chives

After fresh or frozen vegetables are cooked and drained, return
to the hot pan, add the cream and lemon juice to sharpen the
flavour and a seasoning of salt and pepper. Add the parsley or
chives and toss to mix. Allow to warm through but only gently;
do not boil.

Vinaigrette sauce

Serves 4

3 tablespoons sweet pickle relish
2 tablespoons finely chopped
  parsley
½ level teaspoon castor sugar

¼ level teaspoon salt
6 tablespoons vinegar
6 tablespoons salad oil

Combine all ingredients together and whisk well. Add to hot
drained vegetables and toss well to mix. Nice over cooked asparagus, hot broccoli or hot cooked beans.

Blender hollandaise sauce

Serves 4

2 egg yolks
1 tablespoon lemon juice
pinch of salt and pepper
100 g/4 oz butter

Place egg yolks in blender together with lemon juice and seasoning. Cover and quickly blend. Heat butter until melted and
almost boiling then draw off the heat. Turn blender on at high
speed and slowly pour the butter on to egg mixture. Blend well
until thick and fluffy for about 30 seconds. Stand sauce over
warm water until ready to be used.

Serve over cooked broccoli or asparagus.

Mock hollandaise sauce

Serves 4

1 × 75 g/3 oz package full fat soft
  cheese (not processed)
2 tablespoons milk

1 egg yolk
1½ teaspoons lemon juice
dash salt

Blend cream cheese and milk, adding milk gradually. Add egg yolk, lemon juice and salt; beat well. Cook over a low heat, stirring constantly until of a smooth consistency. Serve immediately over hot cooked asparagus or broccoli.

Just for fish

Louis sauce

Serves 4

4 rounded tablespoons
  mayonnaise
3 tablespoons French dressing
3 tablespoons tomato ketchup
salt and pepper

1 rounded teaspoon horseradish
  sauce
1 teaspoon Worcestershire sauce

Combine all ingredients together. Serve with grilled or fried fish, or use as a base for shellfish cocktails.

Quick tartare sauce

Serves 4

4 rounded tablespoons
  mayonnaise
1 tablespoon finely chopped sweet
  pickle
1 tablespoon finely chopped
  parsley

1 tablespoon finely chopped
  capers
1 tablespoon cream or top of the
  milk

Combine ingredients together and warm through gently. Serve with hot or cold fish, delicious with shellfish.

Cucumber sauce

Serves 4

½ cucumber
1 × 142 ml/5 oz carton soured
  cream
salt and pepper

squeeze of lemon juice
1 teaspoon finely grated onion
1 teaspoon chopped parsley

Peel and halve the cucumber lengthwise. Remove centre seeds and finely chop the flesh. Add to the soured cream, along with a seasoning of salt and pepper and lemon juice to sharpen the flavour. Stir in the onion and chopped parsley.

Serve with hot or cold salmon or grilled mackerel.

Quick tomato sauce

Serves 4

4 tablespoons tomato ketchup
1 tablespoon dry sherry
1 teaspoon finely chopped chives
  or shredded spring onions

Combine all ingredients together and heat through gently. Serve with grilled or fried fish, especially good with shellfish.

Mustard cream sauce

Serves 4

125 ml/¼ pint double cream
1 tablespoon prepared English
  mustard
salt and pepper

Lightly whip the cream. Stir in mustard and a seasoning of salt and pepper to taste. Serve with herrings, mackerel or grilled fish.

Sharp sauce

Serves 4

1 × 142 ml/5 fl oz carton soured cream
1 small onion, finely chopped or grated

1 rounded tablespoon mayonnaise
1 tablespoon chopped capers
¼ level teaspoon made mustard
squeeze of lemon juice

Combine together the soured cream, onion, mayonnaise, capers and mustard. Stir in sufficient lemon juice to taste. Serve with shellfish, grilled or fried fish.

Avocado sauce

Serves 4

1 ripe avocado pear
4–6 tablespoons oil and vinegar dressing (see page 110)

1 × 142 ml/5 oz carton soured cream

Halve the avocado pear, remove the stone and scoop out the flesh into a basin. Using a fork, mash until smooth, then stir in the French dressing, soured cream and a seasoning of salt and pepper. Taste and serve with any cold meat or ham, or cold poached fish such as salmon or trout.

Italian meat sauce

Serves 4

2 tablespoons oil
1 medium-sized onion
1 clove of garlic
400 g/1 lb lean minced beef
1 teaspoon salt
freshly ground pepper

1 × 400 g/14 oz can peeled tomatoes
1 × 60 g/2¼ oz can tomato purée
pinch of dried mixed herbs
125 ml/¼ pint stock
125 ml/¼ pint red wine
chopped parsley for garnish

Heat the oil in a medium-sized saucepan. Peel and finely chop the onion, peel the garlic and crush to a purée with a little salt. Add the onion to the hot oil, cover and cook gently for about 5 minutes until the onion is soft but not brown. Stir in the minced beef. Stir to brown on all sides.

Stir the salt, pepper, tomatoes, tomato purée and mixed herbs into the meat mixture. Add the stock and red wine. Bring to the boil. Lower the heat and simmer gently for 40–45 minutes. Stir occasionally to prevent the sauce sticking and add a little extra stock if necessary. The final consistency should not be too thick. Check the seasoning and serve over boiled spaghetti.

Lobster sauce

Serves 2

1 × 213 g/7½ oz can lobster meat
25 g/1 oz butter
1 level tablespoon flour
125 ml/¼ pint single cream

2–3 tablespoons dry or medium dry sherry
salt and pepper
pinch nutmeg
pinch paprika pepper

Drain the liquid from the can of lobster and reserve. Separate the lobster flesh into chunky pieces and discard any sinews or bone.

Melt the butter in a saucepan over a moderate heat, add the flour and allow to cook gently for 1 minute. Do not allow to brown otherwise this will discolour the finished sauce. Gradually stir in the cream, beating well all the time to get a smooth sauce. Add the lobster juice and sherry and bring up to the boil stirring continuously. Season with salt and pepper, then add the nutmeg and paprika. Paprika pepper adds colour only and should not be confused with cayenne, the very hot pepper. Add the lobster meat and allow to simmer gently for 5 minutes. Serve over plain boiled rice.

Creole sauce

Serves 4

2 onions, peeled and sliced
2 green peppers, de-seeded and shredded
1 clove of garlic, crushed with a little salt
2 tablespoons cooking oil

1 × 400 g/14 oz can tomatoes
1 bay leaf
½ teaspoon dried thyme
1 level teaspoon salt
little freshly milled pepper

Add the prepared onion, green pepper and chopped garlic, if used, to the hot oil in a saucepan. Fry gently for 5 minutes to soften the vegetables but do not brown. Stir in remaining ingredients and bring up to the boil. Cover with a lid, reduce heat and simmer for 30 minutes.

Remove the bay leaf and serve over plain boiled rice.

Minute savers

When making a basic white sauce – warm the milk to be added to the roux of butter and flour. It blends in much more quickly and evenly.

To keep a ready-made sauce for some time, cover the surface of the sauce with a square of wetted greaseproof paper close to the surface with the wet side downwards. Stand the base of the pan in a shallow tin of simmering water – this prevents scorching.

To make a brown roux quickly – brown the flour on a baking tray in the oven before making the sauce.

Keep a jar of seasoned flour handy for making sauces. For every 25 g/1 oz flour sift with 1 level teaspoon salt and ½ level teaspoon pepper.

Where cream is added to a sauce at the end of the recipe, always check the seasoning before serving; cream tends to mellow flavours.

Snack meals

In the evening, simple snack meals make less work for the cook. Toast snacks, cheese or egg dishes are a good idea. Keep the main ingredients in the cupboard, then only an extra item need be purchased specially.

Sliced hard-boiled eggs with prawn sauce

Serves 4
4 eggs
4 slices of white bread
butter for spreading
paprika pepper for garnish

for the prawn sauce:
25 g/1 oz butter or margarine
1 level tablespoon flour
150 ml ⅓ pint milk
salt and pepper
1 tablespoon tomato ketchup
1 × 225 g/8 oz can prawns
squeeze lemon juice

Cover the eggs with cold water and bring up to the boil. Cook gently for 5–8 minutes, drain and plunge into cold water and shell. Set aside while preparing the sauce.

Melt the butter or margarine over low heat and stir in the flour. Cook gently for 1 minute. Gradually stir in the milk, beating well all the time to get a really smooth sauce. Bring up to the boil and simmer gently for 2–3 minutes. Season well with salt and pepper and stir in the tomato ketchup, drained prawns and lemon juice. Heat through gently.

Toast the bread slices both sides, butter and top with the sliced hard-boiled eggs. Spoon the prawn sauce over the top, sprinkle with paprika pepper and serve.

Devilled roe savoury

Serves 4

150 g/6 oz fresh soft herring roes
1 tablespoon flour
1 level teaspoon curry powder
salt and pepper
25 g/1 oz butter

dash Worcestershire sauce
squeeze lemon juice
4 slices hot buttered toast
parsley to garnish

Separate the herring roes. Sift together the flour, curry powder and a seasoning of salt and pepper, and toss the roes in this and then fry very gently in the melted butter only a few minutes each side. Add a dash of Worcestershire sauce to the pan along with the lemon juice. Cook for a further minute, shaking the pan to flavour the roes. Serve the roes on hot toast, garnished with a sprig of parsley.

Creamed mushrooms on toast

Serves 4

25 g/1 oz butter
200 g/8 oz fresh button
  mushrooms, trimmed and sliced
½ level teaspoon salt
freshly milled pepper

2 level tablespoons flour
250 ml/½ pint creamy milk
juice of ½ lemon
4 slices buttered toast

Melt the butter, add the mushrooms and fry quickly over a fairly high heat, stirring all the time. Do not over-cook the mushrooms – they should only be fried for 1 minute. Add the salt and pepper and sprinkle over the flour. Stir to blend then gradually stir in the milk and bring up to simmering. Squeeze over the lemon juice and draw the pan off the heat. Spoon the mushrooms over the hot toast slices and serve.

Variation

Sherried mushrooms

Serves 4

Follow the recipe above, adding a pinch of mixed herbs with the flour. Stir in one 125 ml/¼ pint carton single cream, 1 teaspoon English mustard and 1 tablespoon sherry. Heat until simmering then spoon over hot toast slices and serve.

Curried prawns with egg

Serves 4

8 eggs
8 tablespoons milk
salt and pepper
25 g/1 oz butter or margarine

1 level tablespoon curry powder
1 × 225g/8 oz can prawns
4 slices buttered toast
chopped parsley for garnish

Crack the eggs into a mixing basin. Add the milk, a good seasoning of salt and pepper and beat well to mix.

Heat the butter in a medium-sized saucepan; add the curry powder and prawns and heat through gently for 5 minutes. Add the beaten egg mixture and stir over low heat until the egg begins to cook and thicken. Draw the pan off the heat while the mixture is still moist – take care not to over-cook – and dividing the mixture equally, spoon on to the hot toast. Sprinkle with chopped parsley and serve.

Marinated kipper fillets

Serves 4

1 packet 6–8 frozen boned kipper
   fillets
1 small onion
1–2 bay leaves

for the marinade:
salt and freshly milled pepper
1 level teaspoon castor sugar
3 tablespoons wine vinegar
4 tablespoons oil

Allow kipper fillets to thaw until they can be separated, then pull away the silvery skin from the back of each one. Arrange fillets in a shallow serving dish and cover with the peeled onion, cut in thin rings, and the bay leaves.

In a mixing bowl put a seasoning of salt and pepper for the marinade. Add the sugar and wine vinegar and start to mix. Then add the oil. Mix and pour over the kipper fillets and leave to marinate for 6–8 hours or overnight. Serve with thinly sliced brown bread, or crusty bread and butter and a salad.

French ham and cheese fried sandwich

Serves 4

8 thin slices white bread, with
   crusts removed
4 slices ham

4 slices Gruyère cheese
25–75 g/ 2–3 oz butter for frying

On four of the bread slices arrange a slice each of ham and

cheese. Top with a second slice of bread and trim the crusts away from the sides.

Fry the sandwiches in plenty of hot butter. When beginning to brown, turn and fry the second side. Turn several times, adding more butter if necessary, and cook until golden brown and crisp. Cut in half diagonally and serve.

Savoury rarebit

Serves 4

25 g/1 oz butter	salt and pepper
½ small onion, finely chopped	4 slices toast
150 g/6 oz Cheddar cheese, grated	8 rashers back bacon
2 tablespoons milk	1 tomato

Heat the butter in a saucepan and add the onion. Fry gently over low heat until onion is soft and a little brown. Add the cheese and stir until melted, then add the milk and a seasoning of salt and pepper and stir until well blended. Draw the pan off the heat. Top each slice of toast with 2 grilled bacon rashers. Spread the rarebit over the hot toast and garnish with a slice of tomato. Place under a pre-heated hot grill for a few minutes or until bubbling hot and brown. Serve at once.

Crab and cheese toasties

Serves 4

1 × 169 g/6 oz can crab meat	butter for spreading
2 tablespoons mayonnaise	1 packet (4) processed Cheddar
salt and pepper	cheese slices
8 thin slices white bread	

Drain and flake the crab meat, removing all bone and sinews. Add the mayonnaise, a seasoning of salt and pepper and mix well. Toast the bread slices both sides and butter while hot. On four buttered halves spread the crab mixture evenly, top with the cheese slices and place under a moderately hot grill until cheese is soft and mixture heated through. Top each with remaining toast slices; cut in half diagonally and serve.

Tomato and cheese toasts

Serves 4

4 slices bread
butter for spreading
3–4 tomatoes
salt and pepper

little castor sugar
50–75 g/2–3 oz grated cheese
4 rashers bacon

Toast the bread slices both sides and spread with butter. Nick the skins on the tomatoes and plunge in boiling water for 1 minute. Drain and peel away the skins. Slice each tomato thickly and arrange over the buttered slices of toast. Season well with salt, freshly milled pepper and a sprinkling of castor sugar.

Sprinkle thickly with cheese and top with a trimmed bacon rasher; if rashers are long cut in half and place both pieces on top. Place the toast slices under a pre-heated moderately hot grill and cook gently until bacon is grilled, cheese melted and bubbling hot.

Corn fritters with bacon

Serves 4

1 x 354 g/12 oz can whole kernel
  sweet corn
salt and pepper
1 egg

1 rounded tablespoon flour
50–75 g/2–3 oz butter for frying
8 bacon rashers

Drain liquid from can of sweet corn into a basin. Add a good seasoning of salt and pepper, then stir in egg and flour and, using a wooden spoon, mix to a creamy batter.

Heat some of the butter in a pan and add dessertspoons of sweet corn batter. Fry over moderate heat until browned on one side, then flip over and brown second side. Add more butter as necessary to fry all the fritters – makes about eight. Keep fritters warm and fry trimmed bacon rashers quickly, then serve both together. Corn fritters are delicious with fried chicken joints.

Sautéed kidney with bacon

Serves 4

8 lambs' kidneys
seasoned flour
4 rashers back bacon

1 tablespoon chopped parsley
4 thin slices white bread
butter for spreading

Halve the kidneys, snip out the core using a pair of scissors, and roll in seasoned flour. Trim and chop the bacon rashers and fry lightly. Drain bacon from the pan and add the kidneys to the hot bacon fat. Fry gently for about 5 minutes. Add the chopped parsley and bacon and re-heat gently. Toast the bread slices and butter. Pile the kidneys and bacon mixture on top; serve at once.

Spaghetti carbonara

Serves 2

100–150 g/4–6 oz spaghetti
4 rashers bacon
salt and freshly milled black
 pepper

4 tablespoons dry white wine
1 egg yolk
5 tablespoons double cream
grated Parmesan cheese

Add the spaghetti to a large pan of boiling salted water. Boil without a lid until tender – about 12 minutes, then drain at once.

Meanwhile trim, chop and lightly fry the bacon until crisp. Then add the wine, hot spaghetti and a good seasoning of freshly milled pepper and reheat gently.

Draw the pan off the heat and add the egg yolk mixed with the cream. Turn the spaghetti over in the sauce. Taste and add more seasoning if necessary. Turn into a hot serving dish and sprinkle with grated Parmesan cheese. Have extra Parmesan cheese for serving.

Cheese and potato fritters

Serves 4–6

100 g/4 oz Cheddar cheese,
 grated
50 g/2 oz self-raising flour
½ level teaspoon salt
pinch pepper

400 g/1 lb potatoes
2 eggs
oil for frying

Mix together the cheese, flour and seasoning in a medium-sized mixing basin and then set aside. About 10 minutes before serving (leave till last as potatoes will turn black very quickly), peel the potatoes and coarsely grate. Add to the flour and cheese mixture along with the eggs and stir well to mix.

Heat plenty of oil in a frying pan until quite hot then drop heaped tablespoonfuls of the mixture into the hot fat. Fry till golden on the underside then turn and cook second side – takes about 5–6 minutes altogether. This mixtures makes about 8–12 fritters. Serve immediately with grilled bacon rashers.

Quick egg dishes

There are a thousand and one ways to serve eggs for quick meals. Eggs blend well with new young vegetables, sharp or mild cheese, crisp bacon or fresh herbs. They make featherlight soufflé omelettes, delicious served with a savoury sauce, flat omelettes with onion, tomato or green pepper, or scrambled eggs.

Omelettes

Puffy or soufflé omelettes look glamorous enough to serve to guests, while the flat omelette can be made really filling, using your own choice of vegetables or meat, with added herbs and seasonings.

Tossed salads go well with any omelette and in particular the soufflé ones. Try a salad of washed lettuce, tomato, cucumber slices and watercress sprigs – add a little crispness with shredded green pepper or chicory and toss in French dressing. On the other hand, flat omelettes are nice with a hot vegetable, say beans, plain or in a white sauce, peas with fried bacon or onion added, buttered carrots with chopped parsley or sliced fried mushrooms, or with whole kernel sweet corn stirred in.

Soufflé omelette

Serves 2

3 eggs
1 tablespoon hot water
salt and pepper

25 g/1 oz butter for frying
cheese or parsley for garnish

Separate the egg yolks and whites, putting the whites in a small basin and the yolks into a larger one. For best results, warm the larger basin – fill with hot water for 5 minutes before using, then egg yolks will whisk up more quickly. Add the hot water and a good seasoning of salt and pepper to the yolks and whisk until light in colour and thick. Quickly beat the egg whites until stiff, then using a metal spoon gently fold into the egg yolk mixture.

Heat the butter in a 20 cm/8 in omelette or frying pan until bubbling hot. Pour in the omelette mixture and spread evenly over the pan. Leave over low heat to cook gently for 5 minutes, until omelette is puffy and almost cooked through and brown on the underside. Remove from the heat and place under a moderate grill for only 1 minute – just to cook the top surface. If a very soft omelette is preferred omit this stage. Slip a palette knife under one side of the omelette and fold over on to the other. Hold for a few seconds to seal the two halves together than lift out on to a hot serving plate. Cut in half and serve plain, topped with grated cheese or chopped parsley or one of the following sauces.

Creole sauce for soufflé omelette

Serves 2

25 g/1 oz white cooking fat
1 small green pepper, halved and
  de-seeded
1 small onion, peeled and sliced

1 × 298 g/10½ oz can condensed
  tomato soup
3 tablespoons water
1 teaspoon vinegar
freshly milled black pepper

Heat the fat in a small saucepan and then stir in the finely sliced green pepper and onion. Cook gently covered with a lid for 10 minutes, then stir in the tomato soup, water, vinegar and bring to the boil. Simmer for 5 minutes. Add pepper to taste and serve.

Onion sauce for soufflé omelette

Serves 2

50 g/2 oz butter
2 onions, peeled and sliced
25 g/1 oz plain flour

250 ml/½ pint stock or use water
  plus chicken stock cube
¼ pint milk
seasoning and parsley

Heat the butter in a medium-sized saucepan and then stir in the onions. Cover with a lid and cook slowly for 10 minutes, then remove lid and cook quickly until the onions are beginning to turn golden brown. Stir in the flour and cook over the heat for about a minute, before adding the stock and the milk. Bring to the boil stirring all the time and simmer for 1–2 minutes; add salt, freshly milled pepper to taste and little chopped parsley. Serve.

Flat omelettes The bulky flat, or open omelette makes a marvellous meal. Almost any combination of ingredients may be used, these being heated through or cooked in the pan before the omelette mixture is added. The omelette can be turned and browned on the underside or passed under a moderate grill. It is always served flat.

Spanish omelette

Serves 2

4 eggs
1 tablespoon water
salt and pepper
squeeze of lemon juice
25 g/1 oz butter or 1 tablespoon
  salad oil

1 onion, sliced
1 green pepper, de-seeded and
  shredded
2 tomatoes

Crack the eggs into a basin, add the water, a good seasoning of salt and pepper and the lemon juice. Beat well to mix; set aside.

  Heat the butter or oil in a 20 cm/8 in frying pan. Add the onion and green pepper and fry gently until both are soft – takes about 10 minutes. Meanwhile nick the skins on the tomatoes and plunge into boiling water for 1 minute. Drain, peel away the skins and slice. Add the tomatoes to the cooked onion mixture then stir in the beaten egg. Using a fork stir the mixture gently in the pan. The egg quickly sets when touching the hot base of the pan; stirring continuously helps the egg to thicken evenly. When the mixture is beginning to set, stop stirring and allow the underside of the omelette to brown. Turn over using a palette knife or fish slice and brown quickly on the second side. Do not over-cook; an omelette is nicest a little soft. Cut in half and serve at once.

Country omelette

Serves 2

4 eggs
1 tablespoon water
salt and pepper
25 g/1 oz butter

4 rashers bacon
1 small onion, peeled and cut in
   rings
sliced cooked potato (optional)

Crack the eggs into a basin; add the water and salt and pepper. Beat well to mix, then set aside.

Heat the butter in a 20 cm/8 in frying pan. Add the trimmed and chopped bacon rashers, the onion rings and potato if used. Fry gently until bacon is crisp and onion and potato are browned. Pour the egg mixture over the vegetables and stir gently with a fork. When the mixture begins to set, stop stirring and allow underside of omelette to brown. Turn omelette and brown quickly on second side. Serve at once sliced in half.

Onion and potato omelette

Serves 2

4 eggs
1 tablespoon water
salt and pepper
pinch dried thyme
1 tablespoon chopped parsley

25 g/1 oz butter
1 large onion, sliced
2 medium potatoes, peeled and
   diced

Crack eggs into a basin, add water and a good seasoning of salt and pepper. Beat well to mix; add thyme and parsley; set aside.

Melt the butter in a 20 cm/8 in frying pan, add the onion and potatoes and fry gently over low heat until potatoes are cooked and onion is soft – takes about 10 minutes. Season with salt, otherwise the finished omelette could taste a little dull.

Add the beaten egg mixture all at once, and using a fork stir the mixture until beginning to thicken. Stop stirring and allow the underside to brown. Pass quickly under a moderate grill for about 1 minute to set top of omelette. Cut in half and serve.

Anchovy and tomato omelette

Serves 2

4 eggs
1 tablespoon water
salt and pepper
6 tomatoes

1 tablespoon finely chopped
 anchovies
25 g/1 oz butter
chopped parsley for garnish

Crack the eggs into a basin, add the water and a good seasoning of salt and pepper. Beat well to mix, then set aside.

Nick the skins on the tomatoes and plunge into boiling water for 1 minute. Drain and peel away the skins. When adding tomatoes to an omelette it's nicer to remove the skins first; the appearance of the tomatoes is improved since any skins curl up while cooking and spoil the look of the finished dish. Slice the tomatoes thickly and set aside along with the anchovies.

Melt the butter in a 20 cm/8 in frying pan and when hot add the egg mixture all at once. Using a fork stir quickly until the mixture has thickened and is beginning to set. Stop stirring and allow the underside to brown. Before the egg mixture has set completely sprinkle the surface with the chopped anchovies and then arrange the slices of tomato all over the top. Pass under a moderate grill for about 1 minute to cook the surface, sprinkle with parsley, then cut in half and serve at once without turning.

Scrambled eggs A more sensible and quicker way to cook scrambled eggs is to use a large frying pan. Prepare a basic mixture using 8–9 eggs – sufficient for 4 persons.

Scrambled eggs with herbs

Serves 4

9 eggs
125 ml/¼ pint milk
1 level teaspoon salt
freshly milled pepper

3 tablespoons finely chopped
 parsley
2 teaspoons finely chopped chives
25 g/1 oz butter

Crack the eggs into a mixing basin, add the milk and seasonings and beat well to mix. Add the chopped herbs.

Heat the butter in a frying pan over a low heat and when melted, but not brown, pour in the egg mixture. Cook over low heat, stirring most of the time. Use a metal spoon rather than a wooden spoon; this way the mixture doesn't break up so much. Draw the pan off the heat when the mixture is thickened but still moist and not dry. Serve at once.

Variations

With curry Prepare the basic mixture, omitting the herbs, but add 1 rounded teaspoon curry powder. Cook as above.

With ham Prepare the basic mixture, omitting the herbs. Add 100 g/4 oz finely chopped ham to the butter before the egg mixture. Heat through gently then stir in the egg mixture; cook as above.

With mushrooms Prepare the basic mixture, omitting the herbs. Add 100–150g/4–5 oz trimmed and sliced button mushrooms to the hot butter and fry quickly for 1 minute. Stir in the egg mixture and cook as above.

With onions Prepare the basic mixture, omitting the herbs. Add 1–2 small onions, peeled and sliced, to the butter. Fry gently for about 5 minutes until soft but not browned. Then add the egg mixture and cook as above.

With tomato Prepare the basic mixture, omitting the herbs. Plunge 6 tomatoes into boiling water, drain and remove the skins. Cut in half and discard the seeds, then coarsely chop the tomato flesh. Add this to the butter along with a good pinch of dried basil. Heat through gently then stir in the egg mixture and cook as above.

With cheese Prepare the basic mixture, omitting the herbs. Add 150 g/6 oz grated Cheddar cheese to the mixture and cook as above.

Devilled scrambled eggs

Serves 4

8 eggs
125 ml/¼ pint single cream
1 level teaspoon salt
dash pepper
1 level teaspoon dry mustard

½ teaspoon Worcestershire sauce
75 g/3 oz butter
200 g/8 oz button mushrooms,
  trimmed and sliced

Crack the eggs into a mixing basin, add the cream, salt, pepper, mustard and Worcestershire sauce. Beat well to mix and set aside. Heat half the butter in a frying pan over low heat. Strain in the egg mixture and stir over a moderate heat, stirring until mixture begins to thicken but is still moist. Meanwhile fry the mushrooms separately in the remaining butter. Draw the pan off the heat and serve scrambled eggs along with the mushrooms.

Egg and mushroom scramble

Serves 4

1 × 298 g/10½ oz can cream of
  mushroom soup
8 eggs

freshly milled black pepper
25 g/1 oz butter
chopped parsley for garnish

Empty the contents of the can of soup into a mixing basin and stir until smooth. Crack the eggs into the basin and add a seasoning of pepper. Whisk well until blended.

Melt the butter in a large frying pan over low heat. Pour in the mushroom mixture, and cook gently, stirring occasionally, until the mixture has thickened and is beginning to set. Sprinkle with parsley and serve with hot toast fingers.

Variations

Vegetable scramble Follow the recipe above, using 1 × 298 g/10½ oz can of cream of vegetable soup.

Chicken scramble Follow the recipe above, using 1 × 298 g/10½ oz can of cream of chicken soup.

Celery scramble Follow the recipe above, using 1 × 298 g/10½ oz can of cream of celery soup.

Minute savers

*It's worth buying a non-stick frying or saucepan just for scrambled eggs – saves a good deal of difficult cleaning afterwards.

*Never plunge eggs cold from the refrigerator into boiling water – it's a sure way of cracking them. Cover with cold water and bring up to the boil, then cook as required.

*Sprinkle paprika pepper over cheese, or cheese sauce topped snack, before grilling – browns beautifully and instantly.

*To get rid of the very salty flavour in anchovy fillets, soak in milk about 30 minutes before using.

*Always heat any cooked filling to be added to an omelette. Onion, bacon, mushrooms, ham, or cooked potato should be fried or heated gently in butter first.

*When poaching eggs, add 1 teaspoon vinegar to the water before cooking – it helps the white of the egg coagulate quickly and keep a better shape.

Grilling and frying

Both grilling and frying are simple and quick methods of cooking. Both depend on food that cooks quickly and evenly which therefore has to be of good quality. There are lots of ways to make grilled or fried foods more interesting – food may be marinated beforehand, spicy bastes may be used while grilling, or cooked foods may be served with flavoured butters.

In the case of both methods of cooking, high heat should be used initially, then a more gentle heat used to cook the food through. Garnishes are important for food cooked in such a simple manner – parsley sprigs, chopped parsley, lemon butterflies or wedges are but a few suggestions – see page 182 for others.

Meat to choose for grilling

Steak Only the best cuts of meat are suitable for grilling – cheaper cuts tend to become dry and tough when cooked by this quick method.

Choose from the following steaks: Fillet, which should always be cut in fairly thick slices by the butcher, rump, which is best bought in one large piece and then cut into portions after grilling; porterhouse, which is cut individually – many cooks say this is more reliable as far as tenderness goes than any other steak; frying steak, which means anything – whether good quality or not depends on the price; minute or quick-fry steak, which is cut very thinly and then beaten flat to make cooking fast.

Trim away any excess fat from around the meat, season both sides with salt and freshly milled pepper and brush all over with oil or melted butter. Steak should be cooked under a high heat to seal in the juices – then reduce the flame and cook under a lower heat according to the thickness of the meat, first on one side and then the other. Take care not to prick the meat while turning. When the meat is ready a good cook can tell by the 'feel' of the meat. Press the centre of the meat with a forefinger; if the flesh gives easily under the pressure, the meat is rare – very red with the centre still raw. If flesh resists but is still a little soft, it is medium rare – red in the centre and cooked round the edges. If the meat feels firm, then the steak is cooked right through.

Lamb Choose from the following: Best end of neck cutlets, loin and chump chops. Check there are no splintered pieces of bone, especially in the neck cutlets. If serving garnished with a cutlet frill, then trim the fat away neatly at the top of the bone, otherwise it's not necessary. The larger loin chops can be boned; the butcher will do this or prepare them yourself using a sharp knife and cut the bone out of the chop. Curl the chop, wrapping the thinner part round the centre piece of meat. Wrap each boned chop with a thin bacon rasher and secure with a skewer or cocktail stick.

Season with salt and pepper and brush both sides with oil or melted butter and grill. For extra flavour, sprinkle with a pinch of dried thyme, pressing it well in before grilling.

Pork Choose loin chops – sometimes the larger ones have a kidney included as well. Trim fat neatly and, using a small knife, cut slits at 1 cm/½ inch intervals on the fat down the outer edge on a pork chop – helps to prevent buckling while grilling.

Season with salt and freshly milled pepper or Jamaica pepper. Pork chops have a delicious sharp sweet flavour if rubbed over with equal parts castor sugar and dry mustard – about 1 level teaspoon of each is sufficient for 4 chops – the sugar makes them brown nicely, too.

Veal As for pork – loin chops. Trim chops neatly as for lamb. Season with salt and freshly milled pepper.

Chicken Choose joints or small halved *poussin*. It is not necessary to remove the skin from chicken joints before cooking; simply trim away any loose pieces. Ask the butcher to halve the *poussin* for you.

Season with salt and pepper then brush both sides with melted butter or oil – add crushed rosemary or thyme if liked.

Veal, lambs' and calves' kidneys Lambs' or calves' kidneys are the most suitable for grilling; of the two, lambs' kidneys are smaller and more readily available. To prepare the kidneys, remove all the protective fatty tissue from the outside, snip away any core and remove outer skin. Slice into each kidney on the rounded side, cutting almost through but not quite. Open out the kidneys and skewer in pairs on kitchen skewers. Unless skewered, kidneys will curl up too much while cooking. Brush over with oil and season with salt and freshly milled pepper.

Bacon and gammon rashers Back rashers are the leanest; trim away the rind before grilling but no additional fat is needed. Gammon rashers are usually cut about 5 mm/¼ inch thick. Trim away any rind with a sharp pair of scissors and nick the fat at intervals to prevent buckling while cooking. If you like a mild flavour, soak gammon rashers in cold water or milk for about 2 hours; drain and pat dry before cooking. Arrange rashers for grilling with the fat part of each covering the lean part of the next rasher.

Sausages These need no preparation; simply place close together in the grill pan. Brush with oil, to help even browning; do not season.

Times for grilled meats

	Rare	Medium done	Well done
Steak			
1.5 cm/¾ in thick	3–4 mins	5 mins	8–10 mins
2.5 cm/1 in thick	5 mins	6–8 mins	10 mins
3.5 cm/1½ in thick	6–8 mins	10 mins	12–14 mins
Lamb		12 mins	14 mins

Pork and veal chops (must be well done)		15 mins
Chicken joints and poussin		18–25 mins
Kidneys		6–8 mins
Bacon	2–3 mins	4 mins
Sausages		15 mins

Fish to choose for grilling

Hake, cod and haddock Buy either cutlets or fillets. Wash and trim cutlets; pat dry and season on both sides with salt and pepper. Soak in marinade, if used, or brush fish all over with melted butter.

Mackerel and herrings Whole or boned fish are available. Wash and pat the fish dry. When grilling whole mackerel or herring, cut deep gashes in through the skin on the sides to allow the heat to penetrate. Brush mackerel, but not herrings, with oil before grilling. Serve with wedges of lemon.

Plaice, sole and dabs Whole fish or fish fillets can be bought. Wash sole and pull away the black skin – easiest to ask fishmonger to do this for you. Pat dry; brush with salad oil or melted butter. Place under fairly hot grill depending on thickness of fish; grill on both sides. Grill fish fillets on one side only. Serve with parsley butter, or wedges of lemon and chopped parsley.

Salmon, turbot and halibut Cutlets should be cut about 2.5 cm/1 in thick. Trim and season with salt and pepper, brush over with oil or melted butter. Grill under fairly hot grill turning after 10 minutes. Serve with wedges of lemon and watercress.

Trout Brush whole trout with salad oil and sprinkle with salt and pepper. Place under hot grill, turning after 5 minutes.

Kippers and bloaters No preparation needed. Place whole fish under a medium grill; no extra fat or seasoning necessary. Turn once during cooking.

Times for grilled fish

Hake, cod and haddock	
Cutlets	5–7 minutes each side
Fillets	8–10 minutes one side
Mackerel	
Whole	5–8 minutes each side
Herrings	
Whole	3–5 minutes each side
Boned	6–8 minutes one side
Plaice, sole and dabs	
Whole	2–4 minutes each side
Fillets	4–6 minutes one side
Salmon, Turbot and Halibut	
Cutlets	10 minutes each side
Trout	
Whole	5 minutes each side
Kippers	
Whole	5 minutes one side
Bloaters	
Whole	3–4 minutes each side

Marinades for fried or grilled foods

Marinades can add extra flavour to foods such as fish, chicken or veal, or they can tenderize meat. They usually consist of oil and vinegar or lemon juice, with additional flavourings. Spoon over chicken joints, steaks, chops or fish arranged in a shallow china or glass dish 15 minutes to 1 hour before cooking. Leave to soak, turning the food occasionally.

All purpose marinade Mix 3 tablespoons salad oil, 1 tablespoon vinegar (or dry white wine or lemon juice), a seasoning of salt and freshly milled pepper. Add a little chopped onion or crushed clove of garlic, or parsley stalks if you like for extra flavour. Use for chicken joints, chops or steaks.

Egg marinade Ideal to use in any recipe where the meat or fish is to be coated with breadcrumbs before cooking. Blend together 1 egg, 1 teaspoon chopped parsley, little finely grated lemon rind, 1 teaspoon melted butter or salad oil and seasoning of salt and pepper. Beat lightly together with a fork. Use for veal or pork escalopes, white fish fillets or cutlets.

Lemon marinade for fish Combine together 3 tablespoons salad oil, salt and freshly milled pepper, strained juice of ½ lemon and ½ small onion finely chopped. Use for white fish cutlets or fillets.

Marinade for meat Combine together 125 ml/¼ pint salad oil, 1 tablespoon wine vinegar, 1 onion (peeled and sliced), 1 bay leaf, ½ level teaspoon salt and a little freshly milled pepper.

If liked, this marinade may be used to make a sauce to serve with the meat. Use for steak or lamb chops.

Herb marinade for chicken Combine together 3 tablespoons salad oil, 1 tablespoon wine vinegar, salt and freshly milled pepper and ½ teaspoon dried thyme, tarragon or rosemary. Use for chicken joints.

Bastes for grilled foods

Basting food while grilling gives extra flavour and helps prevent dryness. Liquids can be drippings, seasoned butter, vinegar, oil or special sauces. Brush over chops, chicken joints, hamburgers, fish or sausages while grilling and when turning.

Barbecue baste Blend together 2 tablespoons made mustard, ½ level teaspoon each pepper and salt, 1 tablespoon soft brown sugar, 2 tablespoons wine vinegar or lemon juice and 3 tablespoons tomato ketchup. Brush over sausages, hamburgers, chops, steak or chicken joints.

Mustard baste Blend together 1 tablespoon vinegar, 1 tablespoon made mustard and 2 tablespoons brown sugar. Brush over chicken joints, sausages, pork chops and steak.

Butter baste Melt 100 g/4 oz butter and stir in 4 tablespoons bottled meat sauce and 3 tablespoons tomato ketchup. Brush over hamburgers, steak and lamb chops.

Spicy baste Combine together 4 tablespoons tomato ketchup, 1 teaspoon Tabasco sauce, 2 tablespoons orange marmalade, 1 tablespoon finely chopped onion, 1 tablespoon salad oil, squeeze of lemon juice and 1 teaspoon made mustard.
   Brush over pork or veal chops, chicken joints or hamburgers.

Kebab baste Combine together 3 tablespoons soy sauce, 3 tablespoons pineapple juice and 3 tablespoons thin honey. If liked, marinade the kebabs in the baste first then use as a baste as they are cooking. Extra nice if pineapple chunks are used in the kebabs along with the meat.

Butters

Grilled or fried foods, when not served with a gravy or sauce, can be topped with delicious flavoured butters. Prepare the butter several hours ahead, then spoon the blended mixture on to a square of kitchen foil. Shape into a roll – twist the ends like a cracker and chill in the refrigerator until quite firm. Then slice and top each piece of cooked meat just before serving. These recipes make enough for 4 portions. Any butter not used will store in the refrigerator until next time.

Herb butter Blend 2 teaspoons lemon juice and 1 level teaspoon dried mixed herbs with 50 g/2 oz butter. Serve with steak or fish.

Parsley butter Blend a squeeze of lemon juice and 1 tablespoon finely chopped parsley with 50 g/2 oz butter. Serve with steak or fish.

Onion butter Blend 1 teaspoon Worcestershire sauce, ¼ level teaspoon dry mustard and freshly milled pepper, with 50 g/2 oz butter, until creamy. Then add 2 tablespoons finely chopped or minced onion and 2 tablespoons finely chopped parsley. Serve with steak, lamb or pork chops.

Blue cheese butter Blend 2–3 tablespoons crumbled blue cheese and ½ teaspoon made mustard with 50 g/2 oz butter. Serve with steak.

Lemon butter Blend the finely grated rind and juice of half a lemon and 1 level teaspoon castor sugar with 50 g/2 oz butter. Serve with chicken or fish.

Sharp butter Blend 1 level teaspoon dried mustard, dash of onion or celery salt, ½ level teaspoon curry powder and a little freshly milled pepper with 50 g/2 oz butter. Serve with steak.

Mustard butter Cream together 50 g/2 oz butter, ½ teaspoon ready-made English mustard, 1 level teaspoon chopped parsley and squeeze of lemon juice. Serve with steak or pork chops.

Mint butter Cream 50 g/2 oz butter until soft, then gradually beat in 1 teaspoon vinegar. Add 2 heaped teaspoons freshly chopped mint and a seasoning of salt and pepper. Serve with lamb chops or chicken.

Herrings with mustard butter

Serves 4

4 fresh herrings
75 g/3 oz butter
2 teaspoons made mustard

squeeze of lemon juice
salt and pepper

Have the fishmonger clean the herrings and remove the heads. Split each herring open along the belly and rinse under cold water. Pat dry, turn over on to a clean working surface and press down the backbone to loosen. Lift the bone away from the herring flesh.

Cream the butter until quite soft then beat in the mustard, lemon juice and a seasoning of salt and pepper. Spread this mixture over the insides of each herring and fold closed. Cut a few slashes along the sides of the herrings and place under a preheated hot grill. Cook for 3–4 minutes each side and serve with melted juices from the grill pan.

Chicken grill

Serves 4

4 chicken joints
50 g/2 oz butter
½ lemon

salt and pepper
8 rashers of bacon

Wipe the chicken joints and trim away any loose skin. Melt the butter and draw the pan off the heat. Rub the chicken joints over with the cut surface of the lemon, brush with melted butter and season with salt and freshly milled pepper. Remove the grid from the grill pan and line the pan with a square of kitchen foil, if liked, to catch the juice. Arrange the chicken joints in the pan, skin side down and place under a pre-heated moderate grill.

Cook the chicken for 10–12 minutes, then turn skin side up. Baste again and cook for a further 10–12 minutes. Brush with melted butter several times during cooking.

Trim the bacon rashers and arrange in the pan along with the chicken 2–3 minutes before end of cooking time. Serve the grilled chicken joints with the bacon.

Grilled plaice with shrimp sauce

Serves 4

2 whole plaice, filleted
salt and pepper
25 g/1 oz butter, melted

for the shrimp sauce:

2 × 50 g/2 oz cartons potted
  shrimps
squeeze of lemon juice
1 teaspoon finely chopped parsley

Allow 2 fish fillets per person. Rinse and pat dry then season with salt and pepper and brush with the butter. Place under a medium grill and cook for 5–10 minutes without turning.

Meanwhile empty the potted shrimps into a small saucepan and set over low heat to melt the butter. Add the lemon juice and stir in the parsley. Heat through gently; serve spooned over the fish.

Buttered lamb chops

Serves 4

4 lamb loin chops
50 g/2 oz butter
squeeze of lemon juice
1 level teaspoon dried rosemary

1 level teaspoon salt
freshly milled pepper
1 clove of garlic

Trim the chops neatly and set aside. Melt the butter in a saucepan over low heat – take care not to brown. Draw the pan off the heat and add the lemon juice, rosemary, salt and a little pepper. Keep the butter warm.

Meanwhile, remove outer papery coating and crush the clove of garlic. Spear the clove on to a fork and rub over both sides of each chop. Then, using pastry brush, spread half the flavoured butter generously over each chop.

Arrange the chops on the grid of the grill pan and place under a pre-heated hot grill. Grill until the chops are well browned, for about 5–8 minutes. Turn, brush on remaining butter and grill for the same length of time.

Gammon steaks with pineapple

Serves 4

4 gammon steaks, cut about
 5 mm–1 cm/¼–½ in thick
little soft brown sugar

25 g/1 oz butter
1 × 227 g/8 oz can pineapple
 rings

Trim any outer rind from the steaks and snip the fat at 5 mm/¼ in intervals. Rub the fatty part of the gammon with sugar and place a nut of butter on each steak. Place under a pre-heated hot grill and grill for about 7–10 minutes. Turn, rub fat with sugar, baste with drippings and grill second side for about 5 minutes.

Drain pineapple rings from the tin and place a ring on each rasher. Return under the grill until the pineapple is heated through, then serve.

Variation

Gammon steaks with cheese Prepare and grill the gammon rashers as above, omitting the sugar and pineapple. When cooked, cover each steak with a thin slice of Gruyère cheese and return under the grill and cook until the cheese has melted.

Grilled cod cutlets with cheese and tomato

Serves 4
4 tail-end cod cutlets
salt and pepper
squeeze of lemon juice
25–50 g/1–2 oz butter, melted

for the topping:
2 tomatoes
100 g/4 oz grated cheese

Cod cutlets or steaks should be cut about 2.5–3.5 mm/1–1½ in thick; choose tail-end cutlets since they are neater in shape and small.

Rinse, pat the cutlets dry and trim away any fins if necessary. Season with salt and pepper and lemon juice. Brush with butter and place under a pre-heated hot grill and reduce the heat slightly. Turn the fish after 2–3 minutes and continue cooking until the flesh is opaque and comes away easily from the bone – about 10 minutes. Ease out the centre bone from each cutlet when cooked and discard.

Meanwhile plunge the tomatoes into boiling water for one minute, drain and peel away the skins. Halve and discard the seeds then finely chop the tomato flesh and mix with the cheese. Spoon a little of the mixture over each fish cutlet. Replace under the grill until cheese is melted and bubbling and mixture is heated through. Serve at once.

Kebabs

All sorts of tasty combinations of food can be fixed on skewers and grilled. Brush with oil, melted butter or a spicy butter baste while cooking. It's a good idea to buy about 6 long sharp skewers for recipes such as these. Cook and serve the food on the kebab skewers, then invite guests to push the food off on to their own plates, using the prongs of a fork. Serve a tossed salad or cooked rice – see page 126 – with the kebabs.

Devilled kidneys and mushrooms

Serves 4
8 lambs' kidneys
8 button mushrooms

for the mustard butter:
50 g/2 oz butter
2 tablespoons ready-made English
  mustard

Remove all protective fatty tissue from around the kidneys, snip away the core and remove the outer skin. Slice into each kidney on the rounded side, cutting almost through but not quite. Open out the kidneys and skewer in pairs on four skewers, alternating each kidney with a mushroom. Set aside while preparing the mustard butter.

Melt the butter in a saucepan over a low heat – take care not to brown the butter. Draw the pan off the heat and stir in the mustard. Mix well and then using a pastry bush spread the butter generously over the kebabs. Place the skewers under a pre-heated moderately hot grill and cook for 8 minutes, brushing with the baste. Turn, brush again with mustard butter and grill for a further 2–3 minutes.

Liver and bacon kebabs

Serves 4
100 g/4 oz bacon rashers
300 g/12 oz calves' liver, cut into
  two slices
4 tomatoes

for the butter baste:
See recipe on page 79

Cut rinds from the bacon rashers and cut in half. Trim the liver and cut into cubes; roll the bacon rashers round some of the pieces of liver. Thread on to long skewers along with the halved tomatoes. Set aside while preparing the butter baste. With a pastry brush, generously spread the kebabs with the baste. Arrange the skewers under a moderately hot grill and cook for 10–15 minutes, brushing with the butter baste and turning to cook evenly.

Scampi and mushroom kebabs with devil sauce

Serves 4

1 × 225 g/8 oz packet frozen
  scampi, thawed

about 16 button mushrooms
50 g/2 oz butter, melted

for the devil sauce:
125 ml/¼ pint tomato ketchup
2 dashes Tabasco sauce
1 tablespoon Worcestershire
  sauce

3 level tablespoons made mustard
50 g/2 oz fresh white
  breadcrumbs
1 lemon, cut into wedges

Separate the scampi and pat dry. Wash and trim the button mushrooms and then thread alternately with the scampi on to four kebab skewers and brush thoroughly with the butter.

Combine together the tomato ketchup, Tabasco sauce, Worcestershire sauce and the mustard and then, using a pastry brush, spread generously over the kebabs. Pass the kebabs through the breadcrumbs, shaking off excess and then grill under a moderate heat for 5 minutes each side. Serve immediately with lemon wedges and remaining devil sauce.

Quick sauces to go with grilled or fried foods

Cranberry horseradish sauce

Serves 4

1 × 184 g/6½ oz jar cranberry
  sauce
2 tablespoons prepared
  horseradish sauce

Empty the contents of the jar of whole fruit cranberry sauce into a saucepan, stir with a fork until softened and heated through. Stir in the horseradish sauce. Serve with pork chops or gammon rashers.

Apple horseradish sauce

Serves 4–6
1 × 411 g/14 oz can sweetened
  apple purée
3 rounded tablespoons
  horseradish sauce

Combine together the apple purée and horseradish sauce and warm gently in a saucepan. Serve with grilled sausages or pork chops.

Seafood sauce

Serves 4
2 tablespoons tomato ketchup
3 tablespoons salad cream
dash Worcestershire sauce

Combine all ingredients and serve with grilled cod, or halibut steaks.

Cranberry and apple sauce

1 × 184 g/6½ oz jar of cranberry
  sauce
5 level tablespoons sweetened
  apple purée

1 level teaspoon finely grated
  orange peel

Heat the whole fruit cranberry sauce in a saucepan over a low heat, stirring with a fork until softened; stir in the apple purée and orange peel and warm through. Serve with grilled pork chops or gammon rashers.

Gourmet mustard sauce

Serves 4–6
125 ml/¼ pint mayonnaise
1 tablespoon lemon juice
2 teaspoons made English mustard
125 ml/¼ pint double cream

Measure the mayonnaise, strained lemon juice and mustard into a small basin and mix well. Beat the cream until stiff and fold into the mixture. Serve with hot grilled fish.

Frying

With this method of cooking, recipes can be a little more elaborate. Food is cooked quickly in the pan and if liked a sauce may be made in the pan juices. A good cook will have at least one, if not two or three frying pans – choose the heaviest pan you can afford, preferably cast iron. A French sauté pan – a wide shallow pan with a lid – is a good investment; often food initially fried needs further cooking, and sometimes a lid from a large saucepan may be used or failing that a second frying pan of the same size upturned over the top will do.

Choice of foods for frying are similar to grilling with the additions of liver, and veal or pork escalopes. The choice of fat for frying varies – where a high heat is required use vegetable cooking fat or oil, where flavour is important use butter. Watch the heat when cooking unless quick frying is recommended; ingredients cook more evenly and do not stick when heat is medium or low.

Most foods need a little extra protection against the high heat of frying – a coating of seasoned flour or lightly mixed egg and breadcrumbs is sufficient and adds to the finished appearance, too. Serve with any of the butters or quick sauces given in the grilling section that would be suitable. See frying guide below:

Steak Season steak with salt and freshly milled black pepper. Fry in hot butter turning once, time according to taste and thickness of meat. Time: 5–12 minutes.

Liver Buy liver thinly sliced and remove any skin or tough parts. Soak in milk for 1 hour beforehand. Drain and dip both sides in seasoned flour and fry quickly in butter or vegetable fat, turning to brown on both sides. Time: 5–8 minutes.

Sausages Separate sausages – do not prick with a fork since this encourages bursting. Place in a cold frying pan with 15 g/½ oz vegetable fat, lard or dripping and fry gently, turning to brown evenly. Time: 10–15 minutes.

Lamb chops Season with salt and pepper; add a little rosemary, if liked. Fry lamb chops in vegetable fat or dripping, turning to brown both sides. Time: 15–20 minutes.

Pork chops Trim chops and rub both sides with a mixture of 1 level teaspoon each dry mustard and castor sugar, or season with salt, pepper and crushed thyme and dust with flour. Fry in lard or vegetable fat, turning to brown both sides. Cover and cook slowly, turning occasionally. Time: 20–30 minutes.

Pork tenderloin Slice pork tenderloin into almost the centre lengthwise, then cut across into about 4 or 6 pieces. Place pork tenderloin between sheets of wetted greaseproof paper – this way the paper won't stick to the meat. Beat flat with a rolling pin. Dip meat both sides in seasoned beaten egg and then in fresh white breadcrumbs and then fry quickly in butter turning once. Squeeze fresh lemon juice over the meat before serving. Time: 5–6 minutes.

Chicken joints Trim joints; it's not necessary to remove the skin. Season with salt and pepper and either dip in seasoned flour, or first in lightly beaten egg and then in breadcrumbs or alternatively in melted butter and crushed cornflake crumbs. Place in the frying pan skin side down and fry gently in butter, turning to cook and brown evenly. Time: 30–35 minutes.

White fish Cod, plaice or haddock should be trimmed, cut into fillets or cutlets, seasoned with salt and pepper and then dipped in beaten egg and toasted breadcrumbs. Fry gently in butter, turning to brown evenly. Time: 5–10 minutes.

Whole fish Trim fins and scrape away any fish scales. Herring or mackerel can be fried in butter as they are. Trout are nicest dipped in seasoned flour first. Alternatively herring can be boned then opened flat and dipped first in seasoned milk and then in fine oatmeal before frying. Time: Herring or trout 6–8 minutes. Mackerel 15–20 minutes.

Fried liver with aubergines

Serves 4

400 g/1 lb lamb's liver, cut in thin
  slices
seasoned flour
oil for frying

2 large aubergines, peeled
squeeze of lemon juice
chopped parsley for garnish

For the best flavour, liver should be thinly cut and very quickly cooked – over-cooked liver immediately becomes tough, properly cooked liver should still be a little pink in the centre.

Trim the liver, little should be necessary with lamb's liver; on the more coarse livers, certain pieces of gristle need snipping away. Dip both sides in seasoned flour. Heat sufficient oil to cover the base of the frying pan. Add sliced aubergines and fry gently, turning to brown both sides. Add more oil if necessary to fry all the aubergines. Lift from the pan and keep hot. Add the liver slices and fry quickly for about 2 minutes either side.

Squeeze the lemon juice over the cooked liver and sprinkle with chopped parsley. Lift from the pan and serve with the aubergine slices and juices from the pan poured over.

Variations

Crumbed liver Season the sliced liver with salt, pepper and lemon juice. Dip slices first in lightly beaten egg and then in fine white breadcrumbs. Fry quickly in butter for about 3 minutes each side, then lift on to a hot serving platter. Add a little extra butter to the pan, a tablespoon of chopped parsley and a squeeze of lemon juice and pour over the liver.

French style fried liver Cook the liver as before, omitting the aubergine. After cooking, lift the liver from the pan and pour off all but 1 tablespoon of the cooking oil. Add 1 small onion, finely chopped or minced and fry gently for 2–3 minutes. Add a wine glass of dry white wine, raise the heat and boil quickly to reduce slightly in volume. Add a tablespoon of chopped parsley and pour over the liver.

Steak with mustard sauce

Serves 4

4 fillet steaks
50 g/2 oz butter
125 ml/¼ pint dry white wine
125 ml/¼ pint stock or use water
  plus stock cube

½ level teaspoon salt
pinch pepper
1 tablespoon French mustard
1 level tablespoon dried tarragon

Trim the steaks. Heat the butter in a large frying pan, add the steaks and brown quickly on both sides. Reduce heat and cook gently – 5–8 minutes according to taste. Remove from the pan on to a plate and keep warm.

Add the wine to the frying pan, bring to the boil, stirring all the time and scraping the base of the pan well. Simmer rapidly until almost evaporated, then add the stock and seasoning and continue simmering until reduced by half – takes about 5 minutes.

Meanwhile spread the steaks with a little of the mustard and sprinkle with the tarragon. Pour the sauce from the pan over the steaks and serve immediately.

Kidneys in mustard sauce

Serves 4

8 lambs' kidneys
water – see recipe
1 teaspoon vinegar
50 g/2 oz butter
salt and pepper

1 rounded teaspoon flour
125 ml/¼ pint double cream
1–2 teaspoons prepared English
  mild mustard

Remove fat from around the kidneys. Snip out core and with scissors remove skin. Place in a basin with cold water to cover, add the vinegar and leave to soak for 10–15 minutes.

Drain, pat dry and slice thickly. Add to the hot butter in a frying pan and fry gently for 5 minutes – do not over-cook. Then add a good seasoning of salt and pepper and sprinkle over the flour. Stir in the cream and mustard to taste. Bring up to the boil to thicken and draw pan off the heat and serve at once. Nice with hot buttered toast.

Steak with onion sauce

Serves 4

1 piece of rump steak about
  600 g/1½ lb cut 2.5–3.5 cm/
  1–1½ in thick or use frying
  steak
salt and pepper
75 g/3 oz butter

400 g/1 lb onions, peeled and
  sliced
1 tablespoon vinegar
125 ml/¼ pint white wine or
  stock
1 level tablespoon flour
2 tablespoons cream, optional

Trim the steak and season with salt and pepper – best to keep
the steak in one piece and cut before serving. Heat 50 g/2 oz of
the butter in a large frying pan and add the steak. Fry quickly
to brown on both sides, then add the onions and lower heat to
cook meat – 8–12 minutes according to taste.

Lift the meat from the pan on to a hot serving dish and keep
warm. Continue to cook the onions gently if necessary until soft
then stir in the vinegar and white wine or stock. Season with salt
and pepper and bring up to the boil. Cream the remaining butter
with the flour and then add in small pieces to the onion sauce,
stirring all the time until the sauce has thickened and re-boiled.
Draw the pan off the heat, stir in the cream and spoon the sauce
over the steak. Cut steak in portions and serve.

Pepper steak

Serves 4

rump steak, about 600 g/1½ lb
  or 4 pieces of frying steak
2 tablespoons whole black
  peppercorns

50 g/2 oz butter
4 tablespoons red wine

Trim the meat and set aside. Using a rolling pin or a heavy
weight, crack the peppercorns coarsely and press into the surface
of both sides of the meat. Brown quickly in the hot butter on
both sides, then lower the heat and cook for 10 minutes or until
cooked to taste (see page 87). Lift the meat on to a hot serving
platter and keep warm.

Add the red wine – allowing one tablespoon for each serving
– to the hot pan juices. Heat through and then pour over the
meat and serve.

Variation

Steak with sour cream Cook as directed above. Remove steak from the pan and keep warm. Stir in 1 × 142 ml/5 fl oz carton soured cream and heat just to boiling point. Season with salt and pepper and serve immediately along with the steak.

Veal Parmesan

Serves 4

4 veal escalopes	25 g/1 oz grated Parmesan cheese
seasoned flour	50 g/2 oz butter
1 egg, lightly beaten	juice of ½ lemon
50 g/2 oz fresh white breadcrumbs	parsley sprigs for garnish

Ask the butcher to beat the escalopes out. Dip in the seasoned flour. Then pass through the lightly beaten egg and finally coat both sides in the mixed breadcrumbs and Parmesan cheese. Fry in the hot butter for 10 minutes until brown on both sides, turning occasionally for even cooking. Lift the veal out on to a heated serving plate and keep warm.

Add the lemon juice to the hot butter and shake over the heat to mix. Strain over the veal and garnish with a sprig of parsley.

Fried herrings

Serves 4

4 herrings	fresh white breadcrumbs
little milk	50 g/2 oz butter
salt and pepper	lemon juice for garnish

Have herrings cleaned and heads removed by the fishmonger. Split each herring open, place inside downwards on a clean working surface. Press down the back to loosen the bone, turn over and pull away the bone. Rinse herrings under cold water and pat dry. Dip each one, first in seasoned milk and then in the breadcrumbs, keeping fish open flat. Pat coating on firmly.

Place the fish flesh side down in the hot butter and fry gently for about 4 minutes. Turn carefully to avoid breaking and cook on the second side. Squeeze over fresh lemon juice and serve with tartare sauce.

Variations

Herrings in oatmeal with bacon Prepare the herrings as above, dipping them in seasoned milk and then in medium oatmeal. While frying, trim and grill two bacon rashers for each person and serve along with the cooked fish.

Herrings cooked in cider

Serves 4

4 herrings	150 ml/^{1}/$_3$ pint dry cider or dry
25 g/1 oz butter	white wine
1 small onion, finely chopped	salt and pepper

Scrape scales off fish under running cold water. Remove head, slit belly and clean out inside of fish. Wash thoroughly in cold water. Cut off tails and fins.

Melt butter in frying pan and gently sauté onion until soft – about 5 minutes. Add herrings and pour over cider or wine. Season with salt and pepper and bring to the boil. Cover with a lid; simmer with salt and pepper and bring to the boil. Cover with a lid; simmer very gently for 8–10 minutes, turning fish once.

Drain cooked fish on to a hot serving dish and continue to boil liquid until reduced by half. Pour over the herrings and serve.

Fresh trout

Serves 4

4 fresh trout	freshly milled pepper
25 g/1 oz flour	50–75 g/2–3 oz butter
1 level teaspoon salt	1 lemon

Ask the fishmonger to remove the heads and clean out the trout for you. Sift the flour, salt and pepper on to a plate. When ready to serve, roll the trout one at a time in the seasoned flour and add to the hot butter in a large frying pan.

Cook over moderate heat for about 5 minutes, turning them once. Lift out gently on to a hot serving platter. Add the juice of half the lemon to the hot butter in the pan, heat for a moment then pour over the fish. Serve with remainder of lemon cut in slices.

Fried plaice with lemon butter sauce

Serves 4

2 whole plaice, filleted	50–75 g/2–3 oz butter
salt and pepper	juice of ½ lemon
1 egg	1 teaspoon chopped parsley
browned breadcrumbs	

Remove the fish skins; do this by catching the skin at the tail end with salty fingers – gives a firmer grip. Hold the skin against the table surface and using a sharp kitchen knife at an angle, cut the skin from the fish with a sawing movement.

Season the egg and beat lightly. Dip the fish fillets first in the egg and then in browned breadcrumbs. Pat the coating on firmly. Heat 50 g/2 oz of the butter in a frying pan, add the fillets and fry until golden brown on one side. Turn and fry on the second side. Takes about 6–8 minutes in all.

Lift the fillets from the pan, add remaining butter and melt quickly, stir in lemon juice and parsley. Bring up to the boil then spoon quickly over the plaice and serve.

Kidneys in sherry sauce

Serves 4

8 lambs' kidneys	250ml/½ pint chicken stock
50 g/2 oz butter	salt and freshly milled pepper
1 medium-sized onion, finely chopped	2 tablespoons dry sherry
25 g/1 oz flour	chopped parsley for garnish

Using scissors, snip out the white core from each kidney, then pull away the thin covering of skin. Slice the kidneys thinly. Melt half the butter in a frying pan. When hot add the kidneys and fry gently for 2–3 minutes. Remove the kidneys from the pan and keep hot. Add the remaining butter to the pan together with the chopped onion. Fry gently until the onion is tender and a little brown. Replace the kidneys in the pan and sprinkle with the flour. Stir to blend the flour in with the butter and then stir in the hot stock. Mix well and bring to the boil, stirring all the time. Simmer for about 5 minutes, still stirring. When no red juices flow from the kidneys they are cooked through; by this time too the sauce will be a rich brown. Check the seasoning and stir in the sherry. Sprinkle with parsley and serve with rice.

Pork chops with apple

Serves 4

4 pork chops	1 onion
50 g/2 oz butter	salt and pepper
3 sharp-flavoured cooking apples	1 level teaspoon curry powder

Trim the pork chops and add to the hot butter in a frying pan. Cook gently for 5–10 minutes, turning to brown both sides. Meanwhile peel, core and coarsely chop the apples and peel and chop the onion. Lift the pork chops from the pan and set aside.

Add the mixed apple and onion to the hot butter along with a seasoning of salt and pepper and the curry powder. Fry gently, stirring for 2–3 minutes. Then replace the chops in the pan, piling the apple and onion mixture on top of the chops. Cover the pan with a lid and continue to cook gently for a further 20 minutes. Serve the chops with the apple and onion mixture.

Sautéed pork fillet

Serves 4

1 pork tenderloin, sometimes called pork fillet	50 g/2 oz butter
	1 lemon
seasoned flour	

Trim any fat or sinew from the fillet and cut into 3.5–5 cm/1½–2 in thick slices. Beat each piece out until quite flat. Easiest way is on a wet pastry board using a wet rolling pin – the water helps prevent the meat sticking or tearing.

Dip the thin pieces of pork fillet into seasoned flour and then add to the hot butter in a frying pan. Fry gently for 2–3 minutes each side. Draw the pan off the heat and squeeze over the lemon juice. Serve at once with the juices from the pan.

Fried scampi

Serves 4

1 × 225 g/8 oz packet frozen
  scampi, thawed
seasoned flour
1 egg
1 tablespoon lemon juice

1 tablespoon Worcestershire
  sauce
pinch salt
25–50 g/1–2 oz browned
  breadcrumbs
125 ml/¼ pint oil

Separate the scampi, pat dry if necessary and pass through the seasoned flour, then shake in a sieve to remove excess.

In a small basin beat together thoroughly the egg, lemon juice, Worcestershire sauce and salt and then pass the prawns through this; drain and then toss them in the breadcrumbs. Heat the oil in a large frying pan and then fry the scampi in this for about 4–5 minutes, turning until golden brown and crisp. Drain well and serve immediately with tossed salad.

Old-fashioned fried chicken

Serves 4

4 chicken joints
seasoned flour
50–75 g/2–3 oz butter
parsley for garnish

Wipe the chicken joints and trim away any loose pieces of skin. Dip in seasoned flour to coat thoroughly and shake off excess flour.

Melt the butter in a heavy frying pan and add the chicken joints skin side downwards. Fry quickly to brown both sides of the joints. Then lower the heat, arrange joints, skin side down again – the thickest fleshy parts of the joints needs most cooking – and fry gently for 30 minutes in all. Turn occasionally for even cooking but allow most of the cooking time to the skin side of the bird. If liked, cover the pan with a lid to keep chicken joints moist, but remove pan lid for last 10 minutes of cooking time to allow joints to crisp and brown. Serve with the juices from the pan and sprinkle with chopped parsley.

Variations

Spiced fried chicken Add 1 level teaspoon curry powder or mustard powder to every 2 tablespoons flour; use for coating the chicken before frying.

Fried chicken with mushrooms Add 200 g/8 oz trimmed sliced button mushrooms about half-way through the cooking time. Add more butter if necessary.

Fried chicken with onion and green pepper Peel and slice 1 large onion, halve and de-seed 1 green pepper. Shred the pepper finely and add to the chicken along with the onion about halfway through the cooking time. Stir occasionally to cook onion evenly.

Fried chicken with cream sauce When chicken is cooked, lift the joints from the pan and pour away all but 1 tablespoon of the drippings. Replace over the heat, stir in 1 level tablespoon flour and then ½ pint single cream and a good seasoning of salt and pepper. Re-heat till boiling and add a squeeze of lemon juice; check seasoning and serve.

Chicken in lemon caper sauce

Serves 4

75 g/3 oz butter	1 level teaspoon salt
4 chicken joints	½ level teaspoon pepper
200 g/8 oz mushrooms, trimmed and sliced	½ level teaspoon paprika pepper
1 tablespoon capers	1 clove garlic, crushed with a little salt
2 tablespoons lemon juice	

Melt the butter in a large frying pan and brown the chicken joints quickly on both sides. Remove the chicken from the pan and keep on one side.

Add the mushrooms, capers, lemon juice, salt, peppers and chopped garlic to the butter in the pan. Bring to the boil, return the chicken joints, fleshy side downwards, and cover the pan with a lid. Simmer for 30–35 minutes, turning the joints occasionally until the chicken is tender. Serve the joints with the lemon caper sauce spooned over.

Minute savers

*Garlic burns quickly. In a recipe where garlic and onion are fried, first fry the onions until soft then add the garlic and fry only a further few moments.

*Pour hot fat from frying or grilling into an empty used can or small carton and allow to solidify before throwing out – that is unless you wish to keep it for another time.

*Where seasoned flour is used for coating chicken joints or liver or meat for frying, keep any left over and use for thickening a sauce in the pan.

*Dip the chicken joints in beaten egg and then in a packet of breadcrumb stuffing mix. Excellent for baked or fried chicken, adds extra flavour, too.

*When frying in butter, add 1 tablespoon oil; helps prevent the butter from burning too quickly.

*To make an egg go further for coating fish, chicken joints or veal escalopes for frying – add 1 tablespoon oil and beat together.

Salads and relishes

A salad can be a collection of almost any fresh salad vegetables, cold meats, fish, cheese or eggs that you care to put together. Presentation, colour and appearance are very important – a salad should look fresh, colourful and appetizing. Salad dressings make all the difference to vegetables and relishes or pickles give zest to cold meats.

The preparation of salad vegetables is important and care should be taken to preserve their freshness. Never store prepared salad vegetables uncovered in the refrigerator; keep fresh either in plastic containers with sealed lids or in polythene bags.

Lettuce and curly endive Select crisp fresh heads and wash in plenty of cold water. Best way is to dunk the head up and down in cold water to draw out all the dirt. Break apart and separate the leaves, tear lettuce into smaller pieces if liked but never cut with a knife. Shake the leaves in a colander or salad basket, or pat dry in a clean tea towel. Choose from round lettuces or the long, crisp cos variety.

Chicory Cut a thin slice from the base of the chicory then wash heads under cold water. Shake dry. Discard bruised outer leaves. Separate remaining leaves from the head and leave whole or cut across heads in 2.5 cm/1 in slices and separate into pieces.

Celery Separate stalks from the head of celery, scrub clean; trim off base and tops and then shred finely.

Leeks Trim off base and top green part leaving on the white stalk and about 2.5 cm/1 in of the green part. Cut lengthwise with a knife to the centre only and then wash under cold running water to remove all grit. Shred finely.

Tomatoes Wash and cut into slices or quarters. Or cut into attractive tomato lilies by making zigzag cuts round the middle of each tomato with a sharp knife and separating into two neat halves. Sliced tomatoes topped with spring onions or chives are delicious in French dressing.

Radishes Wash thoroughly and trim off tops and tails. Add to a salad sliced or whole. Or make pretty radish roses – using a small sharp knife slit the radish down from the tail end about 4–6 times to form petals. Take care not to cut right through. Leave in iced water to open out.

Cucumber Wash thoroughly and peel thinly, or flute the skin by running the prongs of a fork down the length. Slice thinly across.

Cress, watercress and chives Wash very thoroughly under running water. Use the tops of cress and watercress only, snip off cress with scissors and using fingers pinch off upper parts of watercress. Pick out greenest leaves of chives and leave whole or shred finely.

Garlic Only the merest suspicion should be used in salads. Best way is to crush the clove and rub round the inside of the salad bowl or dish, then discard clove.

Carrots Scrub to remove any dirt. Always use new, young carrots cut into thin matchsticks, or pare off very thin layers lengthwise to make carrot curls. Leave them in iced water to go crisp.

Beetroot Buy them already cooked; slide off the skins using forefinger and thumb and slice or dice the flesh. Serve separately in vinegar or add it last to the salad as the colour quickly stains lettuce.

Mushrooms Select small button mushrooms. Wash in cold water and trim the ends of the stalks. Slice thinly downwards and use raw.

Onions Ordinary onions should be peeled and sliced into rings. Cover with vinegar for several hours before using – this way they crisp up slightly. Spring onions should be well washed, then you should trim off roots and top parts of the green. Use whole or sliced.

Green pepper Slice in half lengthwise. Remove seeds and core then shred flesh and use it raw.

Salads

Simple salads can be made up very quickly using sliced cold meat, ham or tongue, sliced cooked chicken or chicken joints, smoked sausages such as salami, or fish such as herring rollmops, canned or fresh cooked salmon, lobster, crab or tuna.

Garnish with sliced tomato, crisp lettuce hearts, sliced cucumber, sprigs of watercress or sliced or quartered hard-boiled eggs. Serve with a vegetable or rice salad separately.

Tossed mixed salad

Serves 4
1 lettuce
½ cucumber
3 tomatoes
French dressing

Wash the lettuce discarding the outer bruised leaves and shake dry. Peel and thinly slice the cucumber and either slice or quarter the tomatoes. Just before serving toss in the prepared dressing. Any number of other ingredients may be added such as chicory, watercress, shredded green pepper or quartered hard-boiled egg.

Old-fashioned egg salad

Serves 4

1 lettuce	4 tablespoons oil
6 eggs	1 teaspoon Worcestershire sauce
1 large onion, thinly sliced	1 tablespoon finely chopped
1 level teaspoon salt	parsley
freshly milled pepper	2 tablespoons grated Cheddar
2 tablespoons vinegar	cheese

Wash the lettuce and break into leaves. Arrange the leaves over the base of a salad bowl. Cover the eggs with cold water and bring up to the boil. Boil gently for 5–8 minutes then plunge into cold water and remove the shells. Slice when cold and arrange over the lettuce in layers with the onion.

Combine the salt, pepper, vinegar, oil, Worcestershire sauce, parsley and cheese in a basin. Pour over the salad and serve. Nice with sliced ham, cold sliced beef or cooked chicken joints.

Potato salad

Serves 4–6

400 g/1 lb new potatoes	salt and freshly milled pepper
1 small clove of garlic	3 good tablespoons mayonnaise
4 spring onions	3 tablespoons single cream
2 tablespoons finely chopped	few crisp lettuce leaves and
parsley	chives for garnish

Scrub the potatoes and cook in their skins in gently boiling water until just tender – take care not to over-cook, otherwise they break up on slicing. Drain, cool a little and peel off the skins. Cut into neat cubes. Rub a bowl with the garlic then add the potato. Add the sliced spring onions, parsley and a good seasoning of salt and pepper. Thin the mayonnaise down with the cream and add to the potato, mixing the ingredients while the potatoes are still warm so that they absorb maximum flavour. Leave until quite cold then spoon into a salad bowl lined with the lettuce leaves, sprinkle with a few freshly chopped chives and serve.

Serve with cold meat, chicken, ham or herring rollmops.

Marinated mushrooms

Serves 4–6

400 g/1 lb small mushrooms, trimmed
2 tablespoons olive oil

125 ml/¼ pint French dressing
1 clove garlic, crushed with a little salt

Wash, dry and quickly fry the mushroom in olive oil. Drain into a small basin, cover with French dressing and add the garlic. Stand overnight in a cool place to marinate before serving. Serve with hamburgers or cold meats, particularly beef or lamb.

Scandinavian cucumber salad

Serves 4–6

1 medium cucumber
salt
1 tablespoon castor sugar
1 tablespoon wine vinegar

4 tablespoons cold water
freshly milled pepper
chopped parsley for garnish

Wash the cucumber, then slice very thinly with a sharp knife. Layer the slices in a bowl with salt. Leave for 1 hour for the salt to extract the juices. Meanwhile in a glass serving bowl, mix the sugar, vinegar, water and pepper. Now rinse the cucumber slices, drain well and add to the pickling liquid. Sprinkle with chopped parsley and serve.

This salad is nice with cold meats, particularly beef, lamb, chicken or ham. A fork is useful for lifting out the slices.

Coleslaw salad

Serves 6

½ white cabbage heart
2–3 new young carrots
2 dessert apples
1–2 sticks celery

4–5 tablespoons French dressing
3 rounded tablespoons mayonnaise
4 tablespoons single cream

Rinse the cabbage under cold water and remove any outer damaged leaves. Cut in half, cut away the core and then shred the cabbage finely. Place in a large mixing basin and add the scrubbed and coarsely grated carrots, the apples, peeled, quartered and coarsely grated and the scrubbed and finely shredded celery. Toss the salad with French dressing. Leave to chill for 15–20 minutes.

Meanwhile in a small basin thin down the mayonnaise with the cream. Pour over the salad and toss well to mix before serving.

Dutch onion rings

Serves 4

2 medium onions
1 × 142 ml/5 fl oz carton soured
  cream

¼ level teaspoon salt
1 teaspoon lemon juice

Peel the onions leaving them whole. Slice into rings and place in a mixing basin. Cover with boiling water and allow to soak for 2 minutes. Drain and chill.

Meanwhile combine together the soured cream, salt and lemon juice. Add the onion rings and toss well to mix. Chill until ready to serve. Nice with any cold meats or fish.

Tossed green beans and onion

Serves 4

400 g/1lb cooked green beans
1 onion, peeled and thinly sliced
3–4 tablespoons French dressing

salt
4–5 crisp curly lettuce leaves

Combine beans with onion rings in a mixing basin. Add French dressing and toss well to mix; then set aside covered in a refrigerator to marinate for several hours.

Season with salt and serve the marinated beans and onions spooned into the centre of the lettuce leaves. Delicious with cold meats, particularly beef or lamb.

Celery and tomato salad

Serves 4

1 small head of celery
2 leeks
4 tomatoes

1 box cress
French dressing

Remove the stalks from the head of celery, scrub well and shred. Trim and wash the leeks, shred finely and mix with the celery. Pile this over the centre of a large flat plate. Slice the tomatoes and arrange around the edge. Wash and snip the tops off the cress and tuck round the edge of the plate, under the tomato slices.

Prepare the dressing and, and when ready to serve, give it a final mix and spoon over the salad.

Sweet and sour tomatoes

Serves 4

400 g/1 lb tomatoes
3 tablespoons wine vinegar
2 tablespoons water

1 level tablespoon castor sugar
1 small onion, finely chopped
freshly milled pepper

Nick the skins on the tomatoes and plunge them into boiling water for 1 minute, drain, then peel off the skins. Slice the tomatoes and arrange in a serving dish.

Mix together vinegar, water, sugar and onion and pour over the tomatoes. Leave to stand in the refrigerator. Sprinkle with the pepper and serve with cold meats.

Crunchy cabbage salad

Serves 6

½ white cabbage
2 red dessert apples
2 tablespoons seedless raisins

2 tablespoons salted peanuts
125 ml/¼ pint oil and vinegar
  dressing

Remove any outer damaged leaves and cut the cabbage half in quarters. Trim away the stalk and then cut across the cabbage into fine shreds.

Rinse cabbage shreds in cold water, shake dry and place in a bowl. Add the cored and chopped apples, seedless raisins, salted peanuts and toss the whole mixture in oil and vinegar dressing. Pile into a salad bowl and serve with cold meats.

Rice and pineapple salad

Serves 6
200 g/8 oz long grain rice
1 × 225 g/8 oz can pineapple
   rings
2 tablespoons seedless raisins or
   sultanas

for the dressing:
pinch salt and pepper
½ level teaspoon castor sugar
2 tablespoons vinegar
3 tablespoons oil
½ small onion, finely chopped
1 tablespoon finely chopped
   parsley

Add the rice to a pan of boiling salted water, re-boil and cook briskly for 8 minutes until rice grains are tender. Drain and plunge into cold water to cool. Meanwhile drain the pineapple rings from the can and chop coarsely. Drain the cooled rice and mix with the pineapple and raisins or sultanas.

Blend together the seasonings, sugar and vinegar and add the oil, onion and parsley. Mix well and check seasonings. Pour over rice mixture; toss well. Serve with cold meats, poultry or ham.

Main dish salads

Anchovy eggs

Serves 4
6 hard-boiled eggs
50 g/2 oz butter
1 × 50 g/1¾ oz can anchovy fillets

squeeze of lemon juice
chopped parsley for garnish
crisp lettuce leaves

Cover the eggs with cold water, bring up to the boil. Boil gently for 5–8 minutes, then plunge into cold water and remove the shells.

Cut the eggs in half lengthwise and scoop out the yolks. Cream the butter in a basin, add the egg yolks and drained anchovy fillets, forcing them through a sieve. Cream the ingredients adding the lemon juice. Spoon the mixture back into the hollowed out egg whites and sprinkle with parsley. Arrange on washed lettuce leaves and serve with brown bread and butter.

Variation
Tomato stuffed eggs Follow the recipe above, omitting the lemon juice and anchovy fillets and adding instead a good seasoning of salt and pepper and 2 tablespoons tomato ketchup. Serve with sliced fresh tomatoes and green salad.

Ham salad

Serves 4
1 fresh lettuce
8 thin slices of ham

for the salad:
1 dessert apple
1 small head of celery
1 heaped tablespoon sultanas
4 tablespoons mayonnaise

Wash and separate the lettuce leaves picking out the nice centre leaves. Roll each ham slice up with one or two leaves of lettuce and set aside while preparing the salad.

Peel and core the apple and then cut in dice. Separate the stalks from the head of celery, trim and scrub clean. Then shred finely and add to the apple along with the sultanas and mayonnaise. Blend well to mix, then spoon a little on to each plate. Garnish with the rolls of ham and any remaining lettuce leaves.

Curried chicken salad

Serves 4
4 cooked chicken joints
1 small head of celery

dressing:
125 ml/¼ pint mayonnaise
2 tablespoons single cream
salt and pepper
1 teaspoon curry powder
2 teaspoons lemon juice
1 teaspoon tomato purée

Take the meat from the cooked chicken joints and cut into dice. Separate the head of celery, trim and scrub clean then shred and add to the chicken. In a basin combine together the mayonnaise, single cream, a seasoning of salt and pepper, the curry paste, lemon juice and tomato purée. Let stand 1 hour. Add to the chicken flesh and toss to mix. Serve with a green salad.

Seafood salad

Serves 2–3

1 × 213 g/7½ oz can crab,
  lobster or tuna fish
2–3 stalks celery or 1 green
  pepper

1–2 tablespoons lemon juice
3 tablespoons mayonnaise
salt and pepper
crisp lettuce leaves

Drain the canned fish from the tin and break into chunks, discarding any skin or bone. Add the scrubbed and shredded celery or the de-seeded and shredded green pepper, and pour over the lemon juice. Toss well to mix and leave to marinate for 10–15 minutes. Add the mayonnaise, season and toss well to mix, then spoon on to lettuce leaves. Serve with brown bread and butter.

Variations

Crab salad with cucumber Follow the recipe above, using crab flesh and adding ½ cucumber, peeled and finely diced, instead of the celery or green pepper. Serve on a bed of lettuce topped with sliced hard-boiled egg.

Tuna fish and tomato salad Follow the recipe above, using tuna fish. Add 2 hard-boiled eggs, cut in quarters, and 1 tablespoon finely chopped onion.

Arrange 3 tomatoes, thickly sliced, on crisp lettuce leaves and pile the salad on top.

Prawn salad

Serves 4

400 g/1lb frozen prawns
2 tablespoons home-made
  mayonnaise
1 teaspoon chopped shallot

1 tablespoon finely chopped
  parsley
squeeze of lemon juice
crisp lettuce
2 hard-boiled eggs

Allow frozen prawns to thaw – discard excess juice which is inclined to make the dressing too thin. In a basin mix the prawns, mayonnaise, chopped shallot and parsley and add lemon juice to taste. One serving platter is really effective for this salad; arrange a few crisp lettuce leaves over the plate and pile the prawns on top. Sprinkle with a little extra chopped parsley and for a garnish arrange quartered hard-boiled eggs around the sides. Serve with a green salad and slices of brown bread and butter.

Cottage cheese and fruit salad

Serves 4

1 × 225 g/8 oz carton cottage
  cheese
1 × 225 g/8 oz can pineapple
  rings

1 head chicory
4 medium tomatoes

Spoon a little of the cottage cheese on to each of four drained pineapple slices. Serve along with the washed leaves from the head of chicory and the sliced tomatoes.

Variations

Thinly sliced peeled orange, cottage cheese and mustard and cress.

Peach halves, crisp lettuce heart, seedless raisins and cottage cheese.

Cottage cheese, grapefruit segments and endive.

Sliced tomatoes, seedless raisins and cottage cheese.

Soused herrings

Serves 4

4 herrings, with heads removed
125 ml/¼ pint vinegar
125 ml/¼ pint water

few peppercorns
1 bay leaf
½ onion, sliced into rings

Wash the herrings under cold water and scrape away any loose scales with a knife. Trim off the fins with scissors and cut off the tails. Slit the herrings lengthwise and remove the roes.

Place each herring in turn, cut side down, on a clean working surface and press sharply down the backbone to loosen. Turn over and carefully pull away the bone.

Roll up the fillets and place, packed closely together in a 750 ml/1½ pint pie dish. Mix the vinegar and water and pour over the herrings. Add the peppercorns, bay leaf and onion rings. Cover with a greased paper or a lid and bake in the centre of a moderate oven (180°C, 350°F or Gas No. 4) for 40–45 minutes. Allow to cool in the liquid, then drain and garnish with a few of the onion rings. Serve with a tossed salad or potato salad and fresh lettuce.

Danish herring salad

Serves 4

4 pickled herrings
1 small onion
1 dessert apple
juice of ½ lemon

1 × 142 ml/5 fl oz carton soured
  cream
salt

Drain the herrings and arrange flat on a serving dish. Peel and slice the onion and place in a mixing basin. Cover with boiling water and drain after 1 minute. Peel, core and slice the apple and sprinkle with the lemon juice. Add to the drained onion rings with the soured cream and a seasoning of salt. Mix well and spoon over the herrings. Chill before serving. Serve with brown bread and butter, celery and tomato salad.

Salad dressings

Salad dressing can be made using oil and vinegar or lemon juice as a base with added flavouring or a more creamy dressing can be made using mayonnaise, fresh cream or commercial soured cream. If salads are to be served frequently it's a good idea to make up a quantity of oil and vinegar dressing and store in the refrigerator in a screw-topped jar. Shake well before using and use only as much as is required. To make salad dressing using a mix, see page 191.

French dressing

salt and freshly milled pepper
½ level teaspoon castor sugar
2 tablespoons wine vinegar
4 tablespoons olive oil

Add a good seasoning of salt and pepper to a small mixing basin. Add the sugar and vinegar and mix so the vinegar dissolves all the seasonings. Add the oil and mix well. Taste to check the seasoning before serving. If preferred lemon juice may be used instead of the vinegar. Use for tossing fresh lettuce, sliced tomatoes or cucumber, cold cooked new potatoes, carrots or asparagus tips.

Variations on oil and vinegar dressing

Fines herbes dressing Add 2 teaspoons chopped parsley or a mixture of parsley and chervil and a teaspoon chopped chives to the basic dressing. Serve with a green salad or vegetable salad.

Piquant dressing Add 1–2 teaspoons each finely chopped shallot, capers and gherkins to the basic dressing. Serve with potato salad.

Garlic dressing Add ½ clove of garlic, crushed, and 1 teaspoon chopped parsley to the basic dressing. Serve with chicory or endive.

Mint dressing Add 1 teaspoon finely chopped fresh mint to the basic dressing. Serve with potato salad, tomato salad, or a salad made with fresh pears.

Blue cheese dressing Add 25 g/1 oz crumbled Roquefort cheese to the basic dressing. Serve with a green salad to accompany a steak.

Tomato cream dressing Stir 1 tablespoon tomato ketchup and 2 tablespoons double cream into the basic dressing. Serve with fish salads or hard-boiled eggs.

French dressing to keep

Makes ¹/₃ pint

½ level teaspoon salt
freshly milled pepper
1 level teaspoon sugar

4 tablespoons wine vinegar
125 ml/¼ pint salad oil

Measure the salt, plenty of pepper, sugar and vinegar into a screw-topped jar; add the oil, cover and shake well to mix. Store in the bottle and use as required, shaking before using.

Sharp salad cream

1 × 142 ml/5 fl oz carton soured
  cream
3 tablespoons mayonnaise
1 teaspoon prepared mustard

1 tablespoon finely chopped
  parsley
1 teaspoon chopped onion

Combine all the ingredients together in a mixing basin. This salad cream is especially good with chicken salad.

Sour cream dressing

1 × 142 ml/ 5 fl oz carton soured
  cream
salt and freshly ground pepper

2–3 tablespoons oil and vinegar
  dressing (see above)
1 teaspoon chopped chives

Place the soured cream, seasonings, dressing and chopped chives in a small mixing bowl and blend thoroughly. Chill before serving.

Use for tossing cooked or canned flaked salmon or tuna fish or for new potato salad; this dressing is also delicious on a tomato salad.

Blender mayonnaise

2 egg yolks
½ teaspoon salt
½ teaspoon dry mustard
½ teaspoon pepper

2 teaspoons castor sugar
2 tablespoons wine vinegar
250 ml/½ pint olive oil

Put the egg yolks, seasonings and sugar into a blender, and add 1 tablespoon of the vinegar. Using the lowest speed, just blend them together. Remove the centre cap in the blender top and begin pouring the oil very slowly on to the egg yolks, still on the lowest speed. Add the oil very gradually at first, almost drop by drop from the lip of the jug. The mayonnaise will not begin to thicken until the blades are about half covered by the mixture but still continue adding the oil slowly. When beginning to thicken, continue adding the oil in a thin, steady stream, until only about a quarter of it is left. Then add the rest of the vinegar and the remaining oil.

Use the mayonnaise thinned down with a little cream, if liked, to toss cold cooked potato, quartered hard-boiled egg, cooked flaked fish or prepared shellfish.

Cucumber dressing

2 tablespoons wine vinegar
½ level teaspoon salt
dash Tabasco sauce

½ teaspoon grated onion
125 ml/¼ pint double cream
½ cucumber

Measure the vinegar, salt, Tabasco and onion into a mixing basin
and stir to blend. Lightly whip the cream and stir into the vinegar
mixture. Peel and grate the cucumber, drain thoroughly and fold
into the cream. Chill well before serving – it is particularly good
with fish. Use to spoon over cold poached salmon.

Seafood dressing

2 tablespoons mayonnaise
2 tablespoons tomato ketchup
2 tablespoons double cream

dash of Tabasco sauce
1 teaspoon Worcestershire sauce
squeeze lemon juice

Blend all sauce ingredients together. Check sharpness, adding
more lemon juice if necessary. Use for tossing prepared prawns,
lobster or crab flesh – nice with a little diced fresh melon added.

Relishes, pickles and chutneys

Quick little recipes for relishes are useful as they can be made up
and kept in the refrigerator for 2–3 weeks. Serve with cold meats,
ham or chicken.

Fresh cranberry relish

Makes 375 ml/¾ pint
200 g/8 oz fresh cranberries
½ large orange
200 g/8 oz castor sugar

Wash the cranberries, discarding any bruised berries or stalks.
Pare the orange rind very thinly and set aside. Remove all white
pith from around the orange and cut the orange flesh up coarsely
discarding any pips.

Pass the cranberries, orange rind and flesh through the fine
blade of a mincer, or a mouli-grater, into a basin. Add the sugar

and stir until dissolved – the sugar will dissolve in the juice from the berries and orange. Cover the basin or pour the relish into jars and cover and allow to stand for a day. This relish will not keep more than 2 weeks. Serve with chicken or turkey.

To pickle canned fruits

1 × 822 g/1 lb 13 oz can peach halves
75 g/3 oz soft brown sugar
4 tablespoons white malt vinegar

2.5 cm/1 in piece cinnamon stick
2 teaspoons whole cloves
2 teaspoons whole allspice

Drain the syrup from the can of peaches into a saucepan and stir in sugar, vinegar and spices. Bring slowly to the boil, stirring to dissolve the sugar, and simmer for 5 minutes. Add the peach halves, bring to the boil again and simmer for a further 5 minutes.

Draw the pan off the heat and put the peaches and spiced syrup into a dish; cool. Put in the refrigerator for a few hours, or overnight. Serve chilled with cold gammon or pork.

Note: you can prepare this same pickle using tinned apricots or pears.

Chutney peaches

Serves 4
1 × 411 g/14½ oz can peach halves
8 teaspoons chutney

Drain the peaches from the syrup and reserve ¼ pint. Place the halves rounded sides downwards in a shallow round pie dish and pour over the juice. Place in the centre of a moderately hot oven (190°C, 375°F, or Gas No. 5) and bake for 10 minutes, until thoroughly heated through. Remove from the oven and place a teaspoon of chutney in each hollow and return to the oven for a further 5 minutes. Serve hot with curried recipes, grilled pork or lamb chops, ham or gammon.

Ginger pear relish

Serves 4–6

1 × 825 g/1 lb 13 oz can pear
  halves
75 g/3 oz soft brown sugar
150 g/6 oz granulated sugar
grated rind and juice of 1 lemon

1½ level teaspoons ground ginger
¼ level teaspoon ground
  cinnamon
red colouring (optional)

Drain the pears and reserve ¼ pint of the juice. Put the juice
from the pears, sugars, lemon rind and juice, ginger and cinnamon into a medium-sized saucepan. Bring slowly to the boil,
stirring all the time until the sugar has dissolved, then boil for
5 minutes. Add the pears, coarsely chopped, and sufficient red
colouring to make an attractive shade. Cook over a low heat for
25–30 minutes, or until the mixture is thick. Pour into jars, cool
and seal. Keep in the refrigerator for 2–3 weeks.

Serve with cold meats, particularly lamb.

Sweet and sour apricots

Serves 4

1 × 400 g/14 oz can apricot halves
2 tablespoons wine vinegar
1 teaspoon clear honey

Drain the juice from the can of apricots and reserve 4 tablespoons. Measure into a saucepan, add the vinegar and honey and
bring up to the boil. Simmer for 2 minutes, fairly quickly. Add
the apricots and just turn them in the syrup to glaze and warm
them through. Lift out and serve warm with roast lamb, or allow
them to cool in the syrup and serve with cold meats.

Spiced pineapple chunks

Serves 4–6

1 × 851 g/1 lb 14 oz can pineapple
  chunks
250 ml/½ pint malt vinegar
150 g/6 oz granulated sugar

finely grated rind of 1 lemon
8 whole cloves
small piece root ginger, bruised

Drain the pineapple chunks, reserving ¼ pint of the syrup. Put
the pineapple syrup, vinegar, sugar, lemon rind, cloves and gin-

ger into an enamel saucepan and slowly bring up to the boil, stirring to dissolve the sugar. Add the pineapple chunks, lower the heat and simmer for 15 minutes. Drain the pineapple into a jar and return the syrup to the pan and boil rapidly over a high heat for 10 minutes, until syrupy. Remove ginger and pour syrup over pineapple. Cover and allow to cool.

Serve with cold meat, particularly chicken or ham.

Minute savers

*If olive oil becomes solid in the bottle during cold weather, stand the bottle in a jug of warm water – the oil will quickly become liquid again.

*Never toss green salad in oil and vinegar dressing until ready to serve; the acid in the vinegar makes the lettuce go limp.

*Slice the tomatoes with a serrated knife; it's often a good idea to use the bread knife – much quicker and easier for soft tomatoes.

*If soured cream, mentioned in many of the recipes, is hard to buy – use fresh double cream and sharpen with lemon juice.

Vegetables

A smart cook recognizes the importance of serving vegetables – they add colour and flavour to a meal. When time is scarce there are lots of ways of cooking fresh vegetables in half the time and anyway much can be made of those that cook quickly. On the other hand, frozen or canned vegetables are of a high standard and some of the time saved by cutting down on cooking and preparation time can be spent dressing them up with an attractive garnish or simple sauce.

Simple additions to hot cooked vegetables just before serving could include butter creamed with finely chopped parsley, chives or salt and pepper and a squeeze of lemon juice. Alternatively a carton of soured cream, or fresh cream sharpened with lemon juice, either with added chopped parsley or chives and a seasoning of salt and pepper, added to the hot drained vegetables and allowed to warm through before serving, makes an easy sauce.

Quick creamed potatoes

Serves 4
600 g/1½ lb potatoes
salt and pepper
15 g/½ oz butter
little milk

Peel and thinly slice the potatoes. Cover with cold salted water and bring up to the boil. Simmer for 5–7 minutes or until potato slices are tender, then drain. Return to the hot pan and replace over the low heat for 1 minute, just to dry the potatoes. Add a good seasoning of salt and pepper and using a fork, mash up the potatoes thoroughly. Then using a wooden spoon, beat in the butter and just enough milk to make a creamy, smooth mashed potato mixture.

Variations

Mashed brown potatoes Prepare quick creamed potatoes as above but do not beat in the butter and milk. Instead, heat a little butter in a large frying pan and add the potato. Smooth over and fry gently until crispy brown underneath – takes about 10 minutes. Fold over rather like an omelette, slide on to a plate and serve.

Cottage potatoes Prepare the quick creamed potatoes as above and spoon into a shallow fire-proof dish. Rough up the top with a fork and pour over a little extra melted butter. Sprinkle with grated cheese and place under a hot grill until nice and brown.

Quick roast potatoes

Serves 4
600 g/1½ lb large potatoes
hot dripping – see recipe

Peel and scrape the potatoes and trim so the potatoes are even-sized. Cover with salted cold water and bring up to the boil. Simmer for 10–15 minutes to parboil, then drain and leave potatoes until cool enough to handle. Then cut each potato lengthwise in half.

Either place in the hot dripping around a roast or in a separate small roasting tin of hot dripping. Turn in the hot dripping, then replace in the oven or, if not round a joint, place above centre in a hot oven (200°C, 400°F or Gas No. 6) and cook, turning occasionally, for 30 minutes. If around a roast do not add to the dripping until last 30 minutes of cooking time.

Variation

Bake-roast potatoes Select medium or large potatoes; scrub and dry. Then slice in half lengthwise. Melt approximately 25 g/1 oz butter in a roasting tin, and place potatoes cut side down in the tin. Bake in a hot over (200°C, 400°F or Gas No. 6) for 40 minutes or until potatoes are tender.

Two-stage french fried potatoes

Serves 4
800 g/2 lb potatoes
oil for deep frying
salt

Pare the potatoes and cut lengthwise into slices, then cut the slices into strips; don't make the chips too small – about 1 cm/½ in thick. Rinse in cold water and pat dry in a clean teacloth.

Meanwhile heat sufficient oil in a deep fat frying pan until fairly hot – this initial stage of frying should be only to cook through the potatoes and if liked may be done well ahead of serving time. Add the potatoes to the hot fat and cook until potatoes are tender but not browned. Drain from the hot fat; allow the chips to cool. Set aside until ready to use.

When ready to serve, re-heat the fat until very hot. Plunge in the chips and fry quickly until golden brown. Drain, sprinkle with salt and serve.

Cauliflower with parsley butter

Serves 4
1 cauliflower
50 g/2 oz butter
2 tablespoons freshly chopped
  parsley

Cut away the outer green leaves from the cauliflower, then using a knife, break the head into good-sized sprigs. Wash thoroughly in cold salted water then drain. Add to plenty of boiling salted water, re-boil and simmer for 10 minutes or until the sprigs are tender.

Meanwhile melt the butter in a saucepan and when beginning to brown, draw the pan off the heat and add the parsley. Drain cooked cauliflower and arrange the sprigs either back into the shape of a whole cauliflower or neatly on a serving platter. Pour over the hot parsley butter and serve at once.

Provençal tomatoes

Serves 4

4 large tomatoes
1 clove garlic
4 teaspons chopped parsley

salt and pepper
2 tablespoons olive oil

Wash and keep tomatoes whole; cut a slit in the top of each. Crush the garlic, then pound together with the parsley, salt and pepper. Press into the score made on the surface of the cut tomato and brush with the oil. Arrange in a baking dish and grill for about 8 minutes.

Curried fried tomatoes

Serves 4

4 firm tomatoes
salt and pepper
25 g/1 oz flour
½ level teaspoon salt

50 g/2 oz butter
1 level tablespoon curry powder
1 tablespoon chopped parsley

Slice the tomatoes into three, downwards. Sprinkle each side with salt and pepper. Sift the flour and salt on to a plate and dip the tomato slices, one at a time, into the flour, coating both sides well.

In a large frying pan heat the butter and stir in the curry powder. Add tomato slices and fry quickly to brown on each side; sprinkle with parsley and serve.

Fried tomatoes

Serves 4

400 g/1 lb tomatoes
50 g/2 oz butter
1–2 tablespoons castor sugar

salt and freshly milled pepper
little freshly chopped parsley

Wash and fairly thickly slice the tomatoes. Heat the butter in a frying pan, add the tomatoes and sprinkle with the sugar and a good seasoning of salt and pepper. Fry very gently for 15 minutes. Sprinkle with chopped parsley and serve. This is delicious with steaks, fried eggs, or bacon or even on hot buttered toast.

Baked tomatoes with herbs

Serves 4

4 large tomatoes
4 nuts of butter
1 tablespoon chopped parsley

pinch mixed dried herbs
1 tablespoon water

Wash the tomatoes. Using the tip of a knife, run blade around centre of tomatoes to just pierce skin. Arrange in a baking tin with the nut of butter on each, sprinkle with parsley and dried herbs and add the water. Cover with a buttered paper and place on centre shelf of a moderate oven (180°C, 350°F or Gas No. 4). Bake tomatoes for 30 minutes.

Onions and green peppers

Serves 4

2–3 medium-sized onions
1 large or 2 small green peppers
25 g/1 oz butter for frying

Peel and slice the onions. Remove stalks from the peppers, halve and discard seeds from inside. Shred peppers fairly thinly.

Heat the butter in a frying pan and add both onion and pepper together. Fry gently, stirring occasionally for about 10 minutes until onions and peppers have softened and then serve at once. Delicious with steak and chips.

Sweet and sour onions

Serves 4

4 medium-sized onions
25 g/1 oz butter
juice of half a lemon
3 teaspoons castor sugar

Peel and slice the onions. Heat the butter in a frying pan and add the onions. Fry gently for about 5 minutes until onions have softened. Meanwhile strain the lemon juice into a small basin, add the sugar and stir to blend. Pour this mixture over the onions and continue to fry fairly quickly until the onions have browned. Serve at once.

Mustard-glazed onions

Serves 4

400 g/1 lb small onions
salt
50 g/2 oz butter

2 level tablespoons prepared mild
  mustard

Peel the onions and leave whole. Cover with cold water, add a little salt and bring up to the boil. Simmer gently for 15–20 minutes or until onions are tender – test with a sharp skewer or knife point. When ready, drain from the water and in the hot pan melt the butter and stir in the mustard. Add the onions and toss to coat well. Serve at once.

Mushrooms in butter

Serves 4

400 g/8 oz cultivated button
  mushrooms
25 g/1 oz butter
salt and pepper

Wash the mushrooms and trim the ends of the stalks. It is not necessary to peel cultivated mushrooms. Slice the mushrooms and add to the melted butter in a saucepan; cover with a lid and place over a low heat. Shake the pan occasionally and allow to heat through but not to over-cook – takes about 5 minutes. Remove the lid, add a seasoning of salt and pepper and serve at once.

Dress-ups for canned or frozen vegetables

Canned vegetables are nice as they come from the can. Remember that canned foods are cooked foods, and don't throw away the liquid from the can – nothing is added except salt and sometimes a little sugar for flavouring.

When heating commercially canned vegetables follow these directions: First drain the liquid into a saucepan. Boil it rapidly to reduce the amount a little then add the vegetables and heat quickly. Drain, season to taste and serve. Alternatively, the liquid in the can could be saved for soups, sauces or gravies.

Frozen vegetables on the other hand are partially cooked. They should be cooked while still frozen – following the directions and times given on the packets.

Golden broccoli

Serves 4

1 large packet frozen broccoli
1 egg
2 tablespoons mayonnaise

squeeze of lemon juice
seasoning of onion salt

Cook the frozen broccoli as directed on the packet. Meanwhile hard-boil the egg and in a small basin combine together the mayonnaise, lemon juice and onion salt. Spoon the mayonnaise sauce over the hot broccoli and top with the sieved egg yolk. Serve at once.

Broccoli with lemon butter

Serves 4

1 large packet frozen broccoli
25 g/1 oz butter
squeeze of lemon juice

Cook the broccoli according to packet directions. Meanwhile melt the butter in a saucepan until just beginning to brown, draw the pan off the heat and add a squeeze of lemon juice. Drain the cooked broccoli and pour over the lemon butter sauce.

Peas with glazed onions

Serves 4

1 large packet frozen peas
2 medium onions, peeled and
  sliced

1 oz butter
2 level tablespoons castor sugar

Cook the peas according to packet direction. Add the onions to the hot butter in a saucepan and sprinkle with the sugar. Fry gently until onion is soft and golden brown. Drain the peas and add to the pan. Toss well and serve.

Buttered peas

Serves 4
15 g/½ oz butter
1 large packet frozen peas
salt and pepper

Put the butter in a saucepan along with the frozen peas and a seasoning of salt and pepper. Cover with a lid and place over low heat. Shake the pan from time to time so that the peas heat through thoroughly – takes about 5 minutes, then serve at once.

Peas with bacon

Serves 4
25 g/1 oz butter   pinch salt
2–3 bacon rashers, trimmed   1 large packet frozen peas
2 teaspoons sugar

Melt the butter and add the bacon chopped in small pieces. Fry gently until the fat runs from the bacon. Add the sugar, salt and peas. Cover with a lid and cook over low heat, shaking the pan occasionally for 5 minutes. Draw off the heat and serve.

Aubergines and tomatoes

Serves 4
2 large or 3 small aubergines   1 × 397 g/14 oz can tomatoes
salt and pepper   1 teaspoon sugar
1 onion, sliced

Peel, skin and slice the aubergines, sprinkle with salt and allow to stand for 30 minutes. Then drain and place in a saucepan along with the onion, tomatoes plus liquid from the can, salt, pepper and sugar. Cover with a lid and simmer gently for 30 minutes. Serve with steak or chops.

Green beans with almonds

Serves 4
1 large packet frozen sliced green   1 oz flaked almonds
  beans   1 small onion, peeled and finely
25 g/1 oz butter   chopped

Cook the beans according to packet directions. Melt the butter in a saucepan and add the almonds and onion. Fry gently until almonds have browned and onions softened. Drain the cooked beans and add to the saucepan; toss well to mix and serve at once.

Candied carrots

Serves 4

1 × 539 g/1 lb 3 oz can whole
  carrots, drained
2 level tablespoons castor sugar

25 g/1 oz butter
½ level teaspoon salt

Heat the carrots in the castor sugar, butter and salt. Simmer, turning frequently until the carrots are hot and glazed, then serve at once.

Creamy butter beans

Serves 4

1 × 439 g/15½ oz can butter beans
2–3 tablespoons double cream
1–2 rashers crisply fried bacon

pepper
dash onion salt

Heat the contents of the can of butter beans in the liquid from the can. Drain and toss with the cream, bacon, crumbled in pieces, pepper and onion salt. Serve at once.

Mixed vegetables

Serves 4

1 large packet frozen mixed
  vegetables
1 × 400 g/14 oz can tomatoes

salt and pepper
pinch sugar
nut of butter

Cook the mixed vegetables according to packet directions. Drain and empty into a saucepan. Add the tomatoes and liquid from the can, a seasoning of salt and pepper, sugar and butter. Reheat and serve.

Quick rice

Easy one-two-one method for cooking rice

Rice is often an easy alternative to potato; there is little preparation and it cooks quickly. For savoury recipes always use the long grain Patna rice and follow these easy directions.

Measures are easy to remember – 1 cup rice, 2 cups water, 1 teaspoon salt. Any cup will do, provided you use the same one for measuring both rice and liquid. As a guide to quantities remember: 1 teacup rice equals 150 g/6 oz and 1 breakfast cup rice equals 200 g/8 oz.

Basic top-of-cooker method Put rice, water and salt into large saucepan. Bring to boil and stir once. Lower heat, cover with tight-fitting lid and simmer for about 15 minutes without removing lid or stirring. Test rice by biting a few grains and if not tender or if liquid is not completely absorbed, replace lid and cook a few minutes longer. Remove from heat, turn immediately into a serving dish and fluff lightly with a fork.

Oven method Put rice and salt into oven-proof casserole; add 25 g/1 oz butter and the boiling water and stir. Cover with lid and cook in moderate oven (180°C, 350°F or Gas No. 4) for about 40 minutes. Test as above and if not quite cooked or water not absorbed, cover and cook about 5 minutes more. Fluff rice lightly with fork and serve.

Fried rice This is an ideal way of cooking long grain rice. Melt 25 g/1 oz butter in a large saucepan, add 1 finely chopped onion and stir in the rice. Fry over moderate heat, stirring well, until golden brown. Add the boiling water or stock and salt. Bring to the boil, stir once, cover with a tight-fitting lid, lower the heat and cook for 15 minutes without stirring until rice is tender and liquid absorbed. Fluff with a fork and serve.

Pre-cooked rice

American ready-cooked rice only needs reconstituting – follow the simple directions and in five minutes you will have a light tender rice that is never sticky. Always use equal amounts of pre-cooked rice and water, allow 1 teacup for about 3 servings – pre-cooked rice swells up less than the other types. Add salt and butter to the water (see chart below) and bring to boil. Stir in rice, cover with tight-fitting lid and draw pan off boil. Allow to stand for 5 minutes before serving. Fluff hot cooked rice with a fork – never stir with a spoon and serve plain or with the following additions – see below:

To prepare	Rice and water (each)	Butter	Salt
1 serving	$1/3$ teacup	small nut	pinch
3 servings	1 teacup	small nut	$1/4$ teaspoon
4 servings	$1^1/2$ teacups	small nut	$1/2$ teaspoon
6 servings	2 teacups	25 g/$1/2$ oz	$3/4$ teaspoon

Cheese Add 50 g/2 oz grated Cheddar or Parmesan cheese and 15 g/$1/2$ oz butter; toss with a fork to mix. Serve with stews or casseroles.

Saffron Warm a good pinch saffron in a small mixing basin, add a pinch of sugar and crush finely using the end of a rolling pin or wooden spoon. Add 1 tablespoon hot water and infuse for 1 minute. Strain the liquid into the cooked rice and toss with a fork until the grains of rice have taken up the yellow colour. Serve with shellfish or veal.

Mint Add 3 tablespoons mint jelly and 15 g/$1/2$ oz butter to the cooked rice and, using a fork, fold in until combined. Serve with grilled lamb chops.

Parsley Add 15 g/$1/2$ oz butter and 1 tablespoon finely chopped parsley to the cooked rice and toss to mix. Serve with stews, casseroles or curries.

Oriental Add about 2 tablespoons plumped seedless raisins – cover raisins with boiling water for 1 minute then drain and toss to mix. Serve with lamb or curry recipes.

Tomato Add 1 × 227 g/8 oz can tomatoes, drained, and ½ level teaspoon sugar to the cooked rice, then return to the heat and stir for a further 5 minutes. Fluff up with a fork before serving. Serve with shrimps, prawns or any fish recipe.

Rice and peas

Serves 4
150 g/6 oz long grain rice
1 packet quick dried peas
salt

Add the rice and peas together to a pan of plenty of boiling salted water. Re-boil, stirring, then cook rapidly for 15 minutes. Drain and serve the peas and rice together.

Rice au gratin

Serves 4
200 g/8 oz rice, cooked – see
  basic recipes
50–75 g/2–3 oz grated Cheddar
  cheese

Cook the rice following basic instructions. Heap into a hot casserole or baking dish. Add the cheese, toss with a fork and place in a moderate oven (180°C, 350°F or Gas No. 4) for a few minutes until the cheese melts. Serve at once in the casserole dish. Delicious with grilled steaks, chops or fried chicken.

Rice Lyonnaise

Serves 4
200 g/8 oz rice, cooked – see   1 small onion, peeled and finely
  basic recipes   chopped
25 g/1 oz butter

While rice is cooking, melt the butter in a frying pan, add the onion and fry gently for 5 minutes until soft and beginning to brown. Add the cooked rice and stir over a low heat until rice is heated through and well mixed with the onion. Serve with hamburgers, meat loaf or sausages.

Spanish rice

Serves 4

25 g/1 oz butter
1 medium onion, sliced
1 × 400 g/14 oz can peeled
  tomatoes
1 level teaspoon salt

1 green pepper, de-seeded and
  finely chopped
2 teaspoons castor sugar
150–200g/5–8 oz rice, cooked –
  see basic recipes

Melt the butter in a saucepan, add the onion and fry gently until soft and golden brown. Stir in the contents of the can of tomatoes plus liquid from the can, salt, green pepper, sugar and cooked rice. Cover with a lid and simmer for 15 minutes. Serve with chops, steaks and hamburgers.

Rice pilaf

Serves 4

25 g/1 oz butter
1 medium onion, peeled and
  finely chopped
1 bay leaf
150 g/6 oz long grain rice

375 ml/¾ pint hot stock or use
  water plus stock cube
1 level teaspoon salt
pinch pepper
knob butter

In the base of a fire-proof casserole dish, melt the butter and slowly cook the onion until soft, but not browned – takes about 5 minutes. Add the bay leaf and the rice and stir well to coat the grains with the butter. Stir in the hot stock and bring to the boil. Add the seasoning, cover with a buttered paper and a lid and place above centre of a hot oven (200°C, 400°F or Gas No. 6) for 20 minutes. When cooked, remove lid, paper and bay leaf, add a knob of butter and fluff up with a fork.

If a really white rice is preferred, use water and an extra ½ level teaspoon salt in place of the stock.

Rice ring Spoon plain boiled rice or parsley rice while still hot into a buttered ring mould. Pack down lightly, place a serving plate over the mould, turn the right way up and lift the mould away. The rice will remain in a perfect ring shape on the plate. Fill with sauce, curry or creamed mixture and serve.

Minute savers

*Buy a handy runner bean shredder and cut preparation time considerably. As the beans are pushed through, remove outer edges – saves stringing. Cut shredded beans in lengths required.

*Remember that when vegetables are sautéed they will brown if not covered with a lid. When a lid is placed over the pan the steam that collects on the inside of the saucepan lid condenses and returns to the pan keeping the vegetables white.

*Prepare the green vegetables such as beans or sprouts ahead for meals and keep fresh and crisp in a sealed plastic container or closed polythene bag in the refrigerator.

*Always wash a knife used for chopping onions immediately under *cold* water – warm water encourages the smell to stay.

*Butter the inside of a pan to be used for cooking rice with a buttered paper – this way the rice will not stick while cooking and pan is easier to clean afterwards.

Guest appearances

In the corner of a store cupboard always keep a few special items for occasions when friends drop in unexpectedly. Cans of salted nuts, jars of olives, small cans of pâté, sardines or anchovies all keep well. Quick dips or savouries can be made to serve with drinks. If they stay, a simple hors d'oeuvre is easy enough to make and can be followed by a quick main dish with cheese and biscuits, or fruit, or dessert.

Appetizers

Party dip

Makes enough for 12 guests

1 × 225 g/8 oz packet full fat soft cheese
2 tablespoons prepared oil and vinegar dressing
2 tablespoons tomato ketchup
2 teaspoons finely chopped onion
1 teaspoon anchovy essence

In a bowl beat the cheese to soften. Add the oil and vinegar dressing, tomato ketchup, chopped or grated onion and anchovy essence. Mix well to a soft dipping consistency and serve surrounded with crisp salty biscuits.

Avocado dip

Makes enough for 12 guests

2 ripe avocados
1 × 225 g/8 oz packet full fat soft
  cheese
juice ½ lemon

1 teaspoon finely chopped onion
1 level teaspoon salt
dash Worcestershire sauce
2 tablespoons single cream

Halve the avocados, remove the stones and scoop out the flesh into a bowl. Mash the avocado flesh with a fork, add the cheese and beat well to mix. Beat in the lemon juice, chopped onion, salt, Worcestershire sauce and cream and mix to a soft dipping consistency. Serve surrounded with salty biscuits and crisp celery stalks.

Soured cream and sardine dip

Serves 6–8

2 × 120 g/4½ oz cans sardines
1 × 142 g/5 fl oz soured cream
lemon juice

freshly milled black pepper
salt

Remove tails from the sardines, drain well from the oil in the can, and cut them in half and lift out the backbone. Place in a medium-sized mixing basin and using the back of a wooden spoon pound down to a paste. Add the soured cream a little at a time, and then mix well to blend. Stir in a little lemon juice to taste, and add plenty of freshly ground black pepper and salt. Serve in a small mixing basin surrounded with salty biscuits for dipping.

Quick cheese straws

Makes about 36

200 g/8 oz ready-made puff pastry
made mustard
pepper
50–75 g/2–3 oz grated cheese

On a lightly floured working surface roll the pastry out thinly. Spread one half with ready-mixed mustard – best to use English mustard and a little freshly milled pepper. Sprinkle with grated cheese and then fold the other half over.

Roll out to make a little thinner, then using a sharp knife cut first into 5 cm/2 in wide strips of pastry, then into thin fingers. Arrange on a wetted baking tray and place above centre in a very hot oven, 220°C, 425°F or Gas No. 7); bake for 8–10 minutes or until golden brown and crisp.

Salmon paste

Makes enough for 24–36 small
  biscuits
1 × 213 g/7½ oz can salmon
juice ½ lemon
50 g/2 oz butter
salt and pepper

Drain the salmon from the can and remove any bones and skin. Add the lemon juice and mix thoroughly with a fork. Gradually beat into the butter adding a good seasoning of salt and pepper. Blend in a liquidizer if possible.

Use as a spread on small biscuits or squares of toast – garnish with cucumber slices and serve.

Sardine puffs

Makes 36
200 g/8 oz ready-made puff pastry
2 × 120 g/4½ oz cans sardines
cayenne pepper

On a lightly floured surface roll out the puff pastry thinly. Mash the sardines and spread over the pastry. Using a sharp knife cut the pastry into fingers – easiest if you first cut the pastry into strips about 7.5 cm/3 in wide and then across in 2.5 cm/3 in strips. Arrange on a baking tray and place high up in a very hot oven (220°C, 425°F or Gas No. 7) and bake for 10–15 minutes. Sprinkle with cayenne pepper and serve hot.

Petits bouchées au parfait

Makes 12 tartlets

200 g/8 oz ready-made puff
  pastry
1 × 63 g/2¼ oz can Swiss pâté
1 × 125 ml/¼ pint carton single
  cream

1 egg
salt and pepper
pinch nutmeg

On a lightly floured working surface roll the pastry out thinly and using a 5 cm/2 in round cutter stamp out approximately 12 circles. Use these to line small tartlet tins. Cream the pâté until soft and spoon a little into the base of each pastry. Combine together the cream, egg yolk, a good seasoning of salt and pepper and a pinch of nutmeg. Pour into each pasty almost filling them.

Place in the centre of a hot oven (200°C, 400°F or Gas No. 6) and bake for 15 minutes, until golden brown and set. Serve warm.

Parmesan toasties Brush Ritz crackers with melted butter, sprinkle with garlic salt and then grated Parmesan cheese. Bake in a slow oven (160°C, 325°F or Gas No. 3), until hot and golden.

Potato chip canapés Soften liver sausage or canned pâté with a little cream of mayonnaise and drop by spoonfuls on to crisp potato chips.

Smoked salmon canapés Trim away ragged edges and cut slices of smoked salmon to fit thin slices of pumpernickel that have been spread with unsalted butter. Then cut into bite-sized pieces to make delicious canapés.

Stuffed vine leaves Are available in tins so keep some in stock. Turn on to a plate and provide cocktail sticks for spearing them.

Antipasto platter Group together a pretty collection of items that need no preparation. Choose from ripe black olives, paper-thin slices of salami or garlic sausage, chunks of cheese, crisp celery, or slices of smoked chicken.

Celery stalks Fill crisp washed celery with any of the following – taramasalata, liptauer cheese, smoked mackerel or kipper pâté – then refrigerate and cut into bite-sized pieces for serving.

Hot potato chips Heat the oven to moderate (180°C, 350°F or Gas No. 4). Spread 1 packet plain potato chips on a baking sheet and dust generously with garlic or onion salt. Let them heat through for 5 minutes and then serve warm.

Cream cheese and anchovy toast Cut toast into 5 cm/2 in squares. Spread thinly with anchovy paste. Soften cream cheese with a little milk and, using a pastry tube, make a border of cream cheese round each square.

Lobster canapés 1. Chill 1 × 213 g/7½ oz can of lobster. Open, drain and shred meat, discarding any sinews. Combine with 1 tablespoon each tomato ketchup and mayonnaise, and a squeeze of lemon juice. Spread on crackers.

2. Combine 50 g/2 oz butter with 3 tablespoons finely chopped parsley. Season to taste with lemon juice. Spread on small rounds of bread or any other fancy shapes. Top with prepared lobster meat – see above.

3. Soften a 75 g/3 oz package full fat soft cheese with a little milk. Add 2 tablespoons minced chives. Spread on rounds of bread and top with prepared lobster – see above.

Cheese sticks Take pieces of sharp, medium or mild Cheddar cheese and cut into cubes. Top some with small stuffed olives, some with small pickled onions, others with maraschino cherries. Spear both together with a cocktail stick and arrange on a platter.

Salty radishes Wash radishes and trim away large green leaves, leaving a few of the more tender green leaves on. Serve with salt for dipping into.

Melon balls with ham Take a ripe cantaloupe or honeydew melon and make it into balls with a melon baller. Take paper-thin slices of Parma ham, and cut into thin strips. Wrap one strip around each melon ball. Spear with a cocktail stick to serve.

Garlic olives Place one peeled clove of garlic in a bowl. Add 1 tablespoon of olive oil and drained green olives. Toss together and chill for several hours before serving. For a stronger garlic flavour, chop the garlic clove first.

Easy hors d'oeuvre

Sardine pâté

Serves 4
2 × 120 g/4½ oz cans sardines
salt and pepper
100 g/4 oz butter
juice ½ lemon

Drain the oil from the can and spoon the sardines into a mixing basin. Break up with a fork and season with salt and pepper. Add the butter and beat well with a wooden spoon to combine the ingredients. Beat in the lemon juice, then spoon into a small pot or pretty glass serving basin. Spread level and chill until ready to serve. Serve with hot buttered toast.

Crab-stuffed tomatoes

Serves 4
1 × 169 g/6 oz can crab meat   8 small tomatoes
small piece of cucumber   salt
2–3 tablespoons French dressing   4 crisp lettuce leaves

Flake the flesh from the crab meat into a mixing basin discarding any sinews. Peel and finely chop the cucumber and add to the crab meat along with sufficient French dressing to moisten the mixture. Set aside while preparing the tomatoes.

Wash and cut a thin slice from the stalk end of each tomato. Using a teaspoon, scoop out the seeds and soft part from the centre. Sprinkle each tomato with salt and then turn upside down and leave to drain on a plate for 5 minutes.

When ready to serve, arrange two tomatoes on each of four lettuce leaves and spoon the crab meat in to fill each one. Serve with buttered brown bread.

Sardine-stuffed eggs

Serves 4
4 eggs   1 tablespoon cream, mayonnaise or
1 × 120 g/4½ oz can sardines   top of the milk
salt and pepper   8 buttered brown bread slices
squeeze lemon juice

Hard-boil the eggs, remove the shells and slice the eggs in half lengthwise. With the tip of a knife blade push the yolk out of the whites into a mixing basin. Add the sardines, bones and tails removed, and mash the ingredients with a fork. Season with salt and pepper to taste and beat in the lemon juice and cream, mayonnaise or milk.

Cut thin slices off the base of each white half egg to make them steady and arrange on buttered brown bread slices. Reserve pieces of egg white for decorations. Spoon or pipe the filling back into the halves, dividing it equally between each one. Top with slices of egg white, and serve with extra brown bread and butter.

Tuna fish pâté

Serves 6–8

2 eggs
1 × 213 g/7½ oz can tuna fish
50 g/2 oz butter

1 teaspoon freshly chopped parsley
  or chives
salt and pepper
parsley sprig for garnish

Cover the eggs with cold water, bring up to the boil and cook for 6 minutes to hard-boil. Drain, remove shells and allow to cool. Drain the tuna fish from the oil in the can and cream with the butter in a mixing basin until soft. Pass the quartered hard-boiled eggs through a mincer into the mixing basin, or chop very finely and add. Beat the ingredients together to combine, add parsley or chives and a seasoning of salt and pepper. Spoon on to a small serving dish and using a fork shape into a neat pyramid. Decorate with a sprig of parsley and serve with hot buttered toast.

Tomatoes stuffed with cream cheese

Serves 4

8 ripe medium-sized tomatoes
150–200 g/6–8 oz full fat soft
  cheese
squeeze of lemon juice

Scald the tomatoes and peel away the skins. Cut a slice off the top of each and using a teaspoon scoop out the seeds. Sprinkle with salt and turn the tomato cups upside down to drain.

Using a wooden spoon, blend together the cream cheese and lemon juice. Pile the cheese mixture into the tomato cups and replace the lids. Serve with thinly sliced brown bread and butter.

Fresh tomato salad

Serves 4
6 fresh tomatoes
salt and pepper
1 small onion
2–3 lettuce leaves

for the dressing:
salt and pepper
½ level teaspoon castor sugar
1 tablespoon vinegar
1–2 tablespoons oil

Nick the skins of the tomatoes and plunge into boiling water for 1 minute. Drain and peel away the skins. Wash and thinly slice the tomatoes. Spread the slices out in a shallow plate and sprinkle with a good seasoning of salt and freshly milled pepper. Sprinkle over the finely chopped onion and set aside while preparing the dressing.

In a small mixing basin combine together a good seasoning of salt and freshly milled pepper. Stir in the sugar, vinegar and oil and check the seasoning; then pour over the tomatoes. Leave to marinate until ready to serve.

Roll 2–3 crisp lettuce leaves up together, then using a sharp knife shred the leaves finely. Arrange a little shredded lettuce in the centre of each serving plate, then top with tomato slices. Spoon over a little of the dressing and serve.

Eggs stuffed with pâté

Serves 4
6 eggs
1 × 63 g/2¼ can pâté de foie
25 g/1 oz butter

salt and pepper
sliced stuffed olives for garnish
crisp lettuce

Cover the eggs with cold water, bring up to the boil and cook for 6 minutes to hard-boil. Plunge eggs into cold water and peel off the shells. Slice in half lengthwise and with the tip of a knife push the yolks into a small basin. Add the pâté and the butter and blend thoroughly to mix. Season well with salt and pepper and pile the mixture back into the egg white halves. Top with sliced stuffed olives and arrange on a bed of lettuce.

Eggs in tarragon jelly

Serves 6

6 eggs
1 × 440 g/15 oz tin can clear
  consommé

1 level teaspoon gelatine
fresh herbs – see recipe

Poach the eggs in simmering water until just cooked then lift out
with a slotted spoon and transfer immediately to a bowl of cold
water to arrest the cooking and allow to cool. Measure 2 tablespoons of the consommé into a saucepan and sprinkle in the
gelatine. Let soak 5 minutes. Then add remaining stock, heat
gently and stir to dissolve the gelatine. Pour a little in to cover
the base of six individual moulds or ramekin dishes and refrigerate to set. Then garnish with fresh herbs – a leaf or two of
tarragon, chopped parsley or chives – and place a poached egg
(trimmed to neat shape) top-side down in each mould. Pour in
the rest of the consommé to fill each mould and chill until set.
Turn out and serve on crisp lettuce.

French onion soup

Serves 4

2 medium onions
25 g/1 oz butter
2 × 298 g/10½ oz cans condensed
  beef consommé

water – see recipe
salt and pepper
4 teaspoons grated hard cheese

Peel onion and slice finely. Add to the hot butter in a saucepan,
cover and cook gently to soften – about 10 minutes. Then remove
pan lid and let onions brown lightly. Stir in condensed consommé and 1 soup can water. Season to taste with salt and pepper.
Bring to the boil, recover and simmer gently for 15 minutes. Put
a teaspoon of cheese in each soup bowl and pour in the hot soup
for serving.

Grapefruit cocktail

Serves 4
1 × 569 g/1 lb 4 oz can grapefruit
  segments
1 tablespoon crème de menthe

Empty the grapefruit segments and juice into a mixing basin.
Add the crème de menthe and stir to blend the flavour and
colour. When ready to serve spoon the segments into 4 cocktail
glasses dividing them equally and spoon over the juice.

Buttered prawns

Serves 4

50 g/2 oz butter	paprika pepper
1 × 225 g/8 oz packet frozen prawns, thawed	juice ½ lemon

Heat the butter in a frying pan, add the prawns and heat gently.
When hot, sprinkle with paprika pepper and add the lemon juice.
Serve hot with brown bread and butter.

Consommé and soured cream Thoroughly chill 2 × 440 g/15 oz
cans beef consommé. Spoon jellied consommé into chilled soup
bowls. Serve topped with a teaspoon of soured cream and one of
black caviare-style lumpfish roe.

Melon in grapefruit juice Cut a good-sized honeydew melon in
half, remove seeds and scoop out flesh using a melon scoop. Pile
melon balls in individual glasses and pour over concentrated
grapefruit juice (diluted according to instructions) to almost
cover. Chill before serving.

Pears with cream cheese Peel ripe pears and cut in half lengthways
and scoop out cores from centre with a teaspoon. Squeeze over
lemon juice to prevent discoloration. Arrange on crisp lettuce
and spoon flavoured cream cheese of your choice in the centre.
Spoon over oil and vinegar dressing and serve.

Quick main dishes

Soufflé au parfait

Serves 4

50 g/2 oz butter
40 g/1½ oz plain flour
125 ml/½ pint milk
salt and pepper

pinch nutmeg
1 × 225 g/8 oz can Swiss pâté
4 eggs

Melt the butter in a medium to large saucepan over a low heat. Stir in the flour and cook gently for 1 minute. Gradually beat in the milk stirring all the time to make a thick sauce. Bring up to the boil then draw the pan off the heat, add a good seasoning of salt and pepper and a pinch of nutmeg. Remove the pâté from the can and cut into chunks, add to the sauce and stir until melted and blended into the mixture.

Separate the eggs and beat the egg yolks into the pâté mixture. Whisk the whites in a mixing basin until stiff and using a metal spoon fold into the mixture. Pour into a buttered 7-inch soufflé or round baking dish and set in the centre of a moderate oven (180°C, 350°F or Gas No. 4) and bake for 40–50 minutes. Serve at once with a tossed salad.

Sautéed chicken livers

Serves 4

300–400 g/12 oz – 1 lb fresh
  chicken livers
seasoned flour
1 large packet frozen mixed
  vegetables

50 g/2 oz butter
125 ml/¼ pint chicken stock or
  water plus chicken stock cube
1 tablespoon dry sherry (optional)

Cut the livers in half and toss in the seasoned flour. Cook the frozen mixed vegetables as directed on the packet.

Heat the butter in a frying pan, add the livers and fry quickly until brown, turning them often. Add the chicken stock and simmer a few minutes, then add the drained cooked vegetables and heat through a further few moments. Stir in the sherry if liked and serve at once.

Chilled salmon

Serves 4
2 × 213 g/7½ cans salmon
sliced hard-boiled egg, cucumber
  and watercress for garnish

Chill the unopened can of salmon thoroughly. Open, drain the
fish carefully from the can and remove any skin. Arrange the
salmon either on a serving platter or on individual serving plates.
Garnish with sliced hard-boiled egg, cucumber and watercress.
Serve with the following sauce:

Olive celery sauce In a mixing basin combine together 1 × 142
ml/5 fl oz carton soured cream, 2 tablespoons mayonnaise, 3
tablespoons chopped green olives and 2–3 stalks chopped celery.
Chill before serving.

Mushroom and cheese risotto

Serves 4
50 g/2 oz butter
½ medium onion, chopped
3–4 bacon rashers
200 g/8 oz long grain rice
100 g/4 oz button mushrooms

500 ml/1 pint boiling stock, or
  water and chicken stock cube
salt and pepper
50–100 g/2–4 oz grated Cheddar
  cheese

Melt 25 g/1 oz of the butter in a saucepan and add the chopped
onion and the trimmed and chopped bacon rashers. Fry for a few
minutes to soften the onion and draw the bacon fat. Add the rice
and turn in the hot fat, then stir in the boiling stock and bring
to a simmer. Cover pan with a lid and cook very gently for 20–
30 minutes or until rice has absorbed the liquid. Meanwhile trim
the mushrooms and toss lightly in remaining butter. When rice
is cooked check seasoning with salt and pepper, add cooked
mushrooms and half the cheese. Toss lightly to mix and serve
with remaining cheese sprinkled on top. Nice with crusty bread
and a salad.

Minute savers

*To peel skins of tomatoes quickly for hors d'oeuvre, spear each tomato with a fork and hold over a gas flame turning slowly until the skin cracks and can be pulled away.

*To make hard butter soft for spreading quickly – beat in a little boiling water. Use 1 teaspoonful for every 50 g/2 oz butter and blend thoroughly in a mixing basin.

*To heat bread or rolls that are past the fresh stage for serving with snacks or salads, wrap in kitchen foil and place in centre of a moderately hot oven (190°C, 375°F or Gas No. 5); leave to heat through for 15–20 minutes. Keep wrapped in foil until ready to serve.

*Taste recipes as you go along; better to alter the seasoning when preparing recipe than to leave it so late that it's on the table.

*Work tidily and you'll have less clearing up to do afterwards. Set a large paper carton or carrier bag beside where you are working and simply tip all peelings, cans and cartons into this. When cooking is finished, clear away the box or bag.

Desserts

Deciding on a dessert is usually less difficult than choosing a main course. Ingredients are nearly always to hand in the store cupboard. Make sure you have cans of cream, evaporated milk, creamed rice and fruit and a good supply of glacé cherries, angelica and walnuts for pretty decorations.

Some of the quickest and easiest desserts are made with fresh fruit; it's always a good idea to have plenty of apples, oranges and lemons in the house. Fresh fruit and cheese make a very adequate dessert all the year round, but when citrus fruits are available in winter months it is nicer to turn them quickly into something special. During the summer and in the autumn attention can be turned to the marvellous soft fruits and abundance of apples and pears.

Easy fruit desserts

Glazed pears

Serves 4

1 × 440 g/15½ oz can creamed rice

1 × 411 g/14½ oz can pears

2–3 tablespoons raspberry or strawberry jam

squeeze of lemon juice

Dividing the mixture equally, spoon the creamed rice into the base of four individual serving dishes. Top with the drained pear halves, rounded sides up. Warm the jam in a saucepan along with the lemon juice and spoon over the pears to glaze.

Orange compôte

Serves 4
6 oranges
50 g/2 oz castor sugar
125 ml/¼ pint canned orange juice

Peel four of the oranges, keeping them whole and removing as much of the white pith as possible. Then using a sharp knife slice each orange across into about six. Arrange the slices in a serving dish and set aside to chill while preparing the orange syrup.

Finely grate the rind of one of the remaining oranges into a saucepan. Add the strained juice from both along with the sugar and canned orange juice. Stir over low heat until the sugar has dissolved then bring up to the boil. Simmer for 1 minute then draw the pan off the heat and allow to cool slightly. Pour the syrup over the oranges and chill until quite cold.

Apple Anna

Serves 4

3 dessert apples   15 g/½ oz butter
50 g/2 oz soft brown sugar   1 family block vanilla ice cream
2 bananas

Peel, core and thinly slice the apples and place half the slices in a small casserole, and sprinkle with half the sugar. Peel and slice the bananas and arrange over the apple, and then top with remaining apple slices. Sprinkle with reserved sugar and dot with the butter. Replace the lid and bake in the centre of a hot oven (200°C, 400°F or Gas No. 6) for 20 minutes; remove lid and cook for a further 15–20 minutes, until the apple slices are tender. Serve warm, topped with portions of ice cream.

Banana cream

Serves 4

3 bananas
1 × 142 ml/5 fl oz carton plain
  yoghurt
50 g/2 oz castor sugar

juice of ½ lemon
125 ml/¼ pint double cream
few walnuts or grated chocolate
  for decoration

Mash the bananas in a small basin, add the yoghurt, sugar and lemon juice and mix together.

Whisk the cream until thick and fold into the mixture. Spoon into 4 individual serving glasses, top with finely chopped walnuts or grated chocolate and chill until ready to serve.

Apple shortcake

Serves 4

75 g/3 oz plain flour
75 g/3 oz fine semolina
50 g/2 oz castor sugar

50 g/2 oz butter or margarine
2 eating apples, washed and dried

Sift together the flour and semolina into a mixing basin. Add the sugar and rub in the fat. Press half the mixture over the base of a greased shallow 20 cm/8 in round sponge cake tin. Grate the apple, including the peel, over the mixture, then press remainder on top. Place in a moderate oven (180°C, 350°F or Gas No. 4) and bake for 20–30 minutes. Allow to cool for 5 minutes, then cut in wedges and serve with cream.

Baked apples

Serves 4

4 large, sharp-flavoured apples
castor sugar – see recipe
25 g/1 oz butter

3–4 tablespoons water
125 ml/¼ pint single cream

Wash the apples and remove the cores keeping the apples whole. Using the tip of a sharp knife run the blade around the centre of the apple just to pierce the skin. Place the apples in a large roasting or baking tin. Fill the centre of each with sugar and top each apple with a piece of butter. Add the water to the tin and place on the centre shelf of a moderate oven (180°C, 350°F or Gas No. 4).

When baked, the apples will puff up and become quite soft – then serve with the syrup from the tin and the single cream.

Rum bananas

Serves 6

50 g/2 oz butter
6 peeled ripe bananas, cut in half
  lengthwise

50 g/2 oz soft brown sugar
pinch cinnamon
2–3 tablespoons rum

Melt the butter in a frying pan over low heat. Add the bananas, sprinkle with mixed sugar and cinnamon. Fry gently until the bananas are lightly browned, then turn. When the bananas are soft, add the rum, set alight and serve at once with the liquid spooned from the pan.

Peach melba

Serves 6

1 × 225 g/8 oz packet frozen
  raspberries
25 g/1 oz granulated sugar
2 level teaspoons cornflour

1 small block vanilla ice cream
1 × 722 g/1 lb 13 oz can peach
  halves, drained

Turn the raspberries into a small mixing basin, sprinkle over the sugar and set aside to thaw until the raspberries are soft and a juice forms. Spoon the raspberries into a small saucepan and blend the cornflour smoothly with the juice left in the basin. Add to the raspberries in the saucepan, place over a low heat and bring to the boil, stirring continuously until thickened and boiling. Draw the pan off the heat and set aside stirring occasionally until cool.

Place a scoop of ice cream in six individual glasses and top with a peach half rounded side up, and pour over the raspberry sauce. Serve with a pompadour wafer if liked.

Orange fool

Serves 6

125 ml/½ pint double cream
3 medium oranges
1 lemon

75 g/3 oz castor sugar
1 egg white

Finely grate the rind from the oranges and lemon into a small basin. Add the strained fruit juice and the sugar. Stir to dissolve the sugar in the fruit juices.

Pour the cream into a larger mixing basin and add the unbeaten egg white. Whisk the cream until thick and light, then using a metal spoon, fold in the orange and sugar liquid. At first the quantity of liquid may appear to be almost too much, but cut and fold through the cream, turning the basin to get a smooth, deliciously flavoured orange fool.

Pour into six individual glasses and chill for several hours when the mixture will take on a thick texture.

This is a good dessert for a dinner party as it can be made well in advance. Serve with sponge fingers.

Gingered pears

Serves 4

50 g/2 oz crystallized ginger
125 ml/¼ pint water
75 g/3 oz castor sugar
juice of ½ lemon

1 × 822 g/1 lb 13 oz can pear halves
chopped angelica and halved glacé cherries for decoration

Rinse the sugar coating off the ginger under warm water and then chop ginger finely. Measure the water, sugar and lemon juice into a medium-sized saucepan and stir over a low heat to dissolve the sugar. When making syrup for fruit all the sugar crystals must first be dissolved before boiling the mixture, otherwise the sugar grains will crystalize round the edge of the saucepan and make the finished texture of the syrup grainy. Add the chopped ginger to the syrup and bring up to the boil. Reduce heat and simmer gently for 5–10 minutes to make a syrupy sauce.

Meanwhile drain the pears from the can, reserving the juice. Place pears in a glass serving dish. Draw the boiling syrup off the heat and add the pear juice. Allow to cool, then pour over the pears. Sprinkle with the glacé fruits and chill very thoroughly before serving.

Quick fruit salad

Serves 3
1 × 411 g/14 oz can fruit cocktail
3 bananas
1 tablespoon sweet sherry or
  brandy

Combine together the contents of the can of fruit cocktail and
the peeled and sliced bananas. Stir in the sherry or brandy and
serve with cream.

Baked spicy peaches

Serves 5
1 × 822 g/1 lb 13 oz can peach   1 level teaspoon cinnamon
  halves   125 ml/½ pint single cream
50 g/2 oz soft brown sugar

Drain the peaches, reserving ¼ pint of the juice. Arrange peach
halves, cut side up in small baking or roasting tin. Pour the
reserved juice into the base of the pan.

Combine together the brown sugar and cinnamon and sprinkle
evenly over the peaches. Bake in the centre of a moderately hot
oven (190°C, 375°F or Gas No. 5) for 15 minutes. Serve at once
with juices from the baking dish, and cream.

Hot pears with ice cream

Serves 4
50 g/2 oz butter   ¼ level teaspoon ground ginger
50 g/2 oz soft brown sugar   1 × 822 g/1 lb 13 oz can pear
½ level teaspoon ground   halves (about 10 halves)
  cinnamon   1 block vanilla ice cream
¼ level teaspoon ground nutmeg

Measure the butter, sugar and spices into a frying pan; drain the
pear halves and arrange over the top. Set aside until ready to
serve.

About 10 minutes before serving, place the pan over a moderate heat and simmer the pears gently for 5 minutes, then turn
over and simmer for a further 5 minutes until heated through.

Place a scoop of vanilla ice cream in 4 individual glasses and place two pear halves on top with a little of the hot sauce from the pan spooned over. Serve at once.

Apple Fool

Serves 4

1 × 411 g/14½ oz can sweetened apple purée

3 level tablespoons soft brown sugar

250 ml/½ pint double cream

toasted flaked almonds for decoration

Spoon the apple purée into a mixing basin and stir in the sugar. Whip the cream until stiff and fold into the mixture; pour into 4 individual serving glasses and top with the flaked almonds. Chill until ready to serve.

Brandied peaches

Serves 4

1 × 822 g/1 lb 13 oz can peach halves

2 tablespoons brandy

few drops almond essence

50 g/2 oz ratafia or boudoir biscuits

25 g/1 oz ground almonds

15 g/¼ oz castor sugar

Drain the peaches from the syrup and arrange cut side up in a baking dish. Reserve about 125 ml/¼ pint syrup and stir in the brandy and almond essence.

Crush the biscuits with a rolling pin and place in a mixing basin with the ground almonds. Mix to a paste with sufficient of the fruit syrup mixture and then place a spoonful of the mixture in each peach hollow. Pour round remaining syrup and sprinkle the castor sugar over the tops of the peaches.

Place above centre in a moderately hot oven (190°C, 375°F, or Gas No. 5 for 20–25 minutes, until the sugar has slightly melted. Serve the peaches warm, with syrup from the baking dish.

Sautéed bananas and pineapple

Serves 4

50 g/2 oz butter
3 medium-sized bananas
1 × 440 g/15 oz can pineapple
  chunks, drained

50 g/2 oz soft brown sugar
¼ level teaspoon ground
  cinnamon
125 ml/¼ pint single cream

Melt the butter in a medium-sized frying pan over a low heat. Peel the bananas, cut into 2.5 cm/1 in chunks and add to the butter along with the pineapple chunks.

Sprinkle the mixed brown sugar and cinnamon over the top and place over a low heat – a high heat might caramelize the butter and sugar. Cook gently for about 5 minutes, turning the fruit occasionally with a wooden spoon, until thoroughly warmed through. Cooked banana turns brown and soft very quickly so serve immediately with a little of the sauce from the pan spooned over and cream.

Apple sponge

Serves 4

400 g/1 lb cooking or sharp-
  flavoured apples
2–3 level tablespoons castor sugar

1 packet of 4 trifle sponge cakes
2 eggs
250 ml/½ pint of milk

Peel, quarter and cut away the core from the apples, then slice fairly thinly. Arrange the apples over the base of a 750 ml –1 litre/1½ – 2 pint baking or pie dish and sprinkle with the sugar.

Separate the sponge cakes and slice each one in half across. Arrange over the apples cut sides downwards – if the dish is a wide shallow one it will be easier to put all the cakes in. Whisk together the eggs and milk and then strain over the cake. Place in the centre of a moderate oven (180°C, 350°F or Gas No. 4) and bake for 1 hour.

More dessert recipes

Quick mousses, jellies and cream desserts can be prepared ahead and left to chill. Use packet jellies as a base for some recipes. For others with gelatine, avoid using too many basins by soaking and dissolving the gelatine powder in a fairly large saucepan, then stirring or folding in other ingredients. Use instant whip for quick trifles or vary them by folding in fruit purée to make fruit fools or whipped cream, chocolate or nuts to make easy cream desserts.

Swiss cream

Serves 6

1 packet lemon jelly
250 ml/½ pint water
1 banana, sliced
few pieces of angelica

1 jam-filled Swiss roll
1 small can evaporated milk
1 tablespoon lemon juice

Dissolve the jelly in hot water to make 250 ml/½ pint, then allow to cool until just warm. Pour enough into a 15 cm/6 in deep cake tin to cover the base and leave to set.

Arrange the banana slices and the pieces of angelica over the set jelly in a decorative pattern. Spoon over a little more jelly and leave to set. Slice the Swiss roll into eight and dip each slice, cut side down, into remaining jelly. Place slices, jelly-coated sides outside, around the edge of the tin. Press well against the sides of the tin and leave to set.

Beat the evaporated milk and lemon juice together until thick. Gradually beat in the remainder of the jelly which should be almost set by now.

Pour this mixture into the centre of the prepared tin and leave in a cool place until set quite firm. Unmould carefully on to a plate and serve with fresh cream.

Fruit jelly

Serves 4

1 lemon jelly
250 ml/½ pint water
1 × 411g/14½ oz can fruit cocktail

Make the jelly up with the water, according to packet directions, and set aside until cool and beginning to set. Stir in the contents of the can of fruit cocktail along with the juice. Pour into a serving dish and leave in a cool place to set. Stir once when jelly is almost setting to get even distribution of the fruit.

Orange and banana jelly

Serves 4–6
Orange squash – see recipe
water – see recipe
15 g/½ oz powdered gelatine
2 bananas

Dilute the orange squash to taste with water and make up 500 ml/1 pint of liquid. Measure the powdered gelatine into a saucepan, add 125 ml/¼ pint of the liquid and allow to soak for 5 minutes. Place the saucepan over very low heat and stir to dissolve the gelatine. Draw the pan off the heat and stir in remaining liquid. Pour the jelly into a serving dish and put to chill until almost setting.

Quickly slice the bananas and stir into the jelly, then leave until set quite firm.

Banana mousse

Serves 4–6
250 ml/½ pint water
1 packet lemon or lime jelly
3 large bananas
juice of ½ lemon

250 ml/½ pint double cream
toasted almonds or grated
    chocolate for decoration

Measure 125 ml/¼ pint of the water into a saucepan, bring up to the boil and then draw off the heat. Add the jelly in pieces and stir until dissolved – the heat of the pan is sufficient to do this. When jelly is dissolved, stir in remaining cold water and set aside until cooled and beginning to thicken.

Meanwhile peel and mash the bananas with the lemon juice. Whisk the cream until thick and then fold into the almost set jelly along with the mashed banana. Pour into a serving dish and leave until set firm. Sprinkle with almonds or chocolate and serve.

Banana custard

Serves 4
3 level tablespoons custard powder
500 ml/1 pint milk
50 g/2 oz castor sugar
2 bananas

Blend the custard powder with a little of the milk to make a thin paste. Heat remaining milk and stir into blended custard. Pour back into the milk saucepan and bring up to the boil, stirring all the time. Draw the pan off the heat, and stir in the sugar and sliced bananas.

Dividing the mixture equally, pour into four individual serving dishes and serve with top of the milk.

Lemon crumb freeze

Serves 8

50 g/2 oz cornflake crumbs
50 g/2 oz castor sugar
50 g/2 oz butter or margarine, melted
2 eggs, separated

1 small can condensed milk
125 ml/¼ pint double cream
finely grated rind and juice of 2 lemons
25 g/1 oz castor sugar

Measure the crumbs into a medium-sized basin and add the sugar; using a fork, stir in the melted fat until all the crumbs are coated. Reserving 2 tablespoons of the crumb mixture for the top, pat the remainder out firmly on the base of an ice cube tray (use large ice tray, if possible) previously lined with a strip of waxed paper. Set aside to chill while preparing the filling.

Combine together the egg yolks, condensed milk and cream. Add the lemon rind and strained juice and stir until thickened.

Beat the egg whites until foamy and whisk in the sugar. Fold gently into the lemon mixture and pour over the base of crumbs in the ice cube tray. Sprinkle reserved crumble over the lemon and freeze for 2–3 hours until firm. To serve, loosen sides and lift out the dessert and cut in slices.

Ginger cream roll

Serves 6

1 × 225 g/8 oz packet ginger
  snaps
250 ml/½ pint double cream
1 teaspoon vanilla essence

chopped candied ginger for
  decoration

Unwrap the ginger snaps and set aside any broken ones. Whip
the cream and vanilla essence until thick and using half the
cream, spread on the ginger snaps and pile on top of each other.
Lay roll on side in serving dish and spoon remaining cream over
and with the tip of a knife spread evenly to cover.

Set aside to chill in a refrigerator for at least 3–4 hours to allow
the biscuits to soften before serving. Sprinkle with candied ginger
and serve sliced diagonally.

Quick chocolate mousse

Serves 4

100 g/4 oz plain chocolate
15 g/½ oz butter
4 eggs
1 tablespoon brandy (optional)

Break the chocolate into a mixing basin and set over a pan of hot
water. Stir until melted and smooth, then add the butter, egg
yolks and brandy, if used. Stir until blended then remove basin
from heat. Stiffly whisk the egg whites and fold them carefully
into chocolate mixture. Spoon into 4 individual serving glasses
and chill until set firm – takes 1–2 hours.

Butterscotch pudding

Serves 4

100 g/4 oz castor sugar
1 tablespoon water
5 level tablespoons custard
  powder or cornflour

500 ml/1 pint milk
chopped nuts for decoration

Measure the sugar into a small heavy saucepan and place over
moderate heat. Stir until the sugar has dissolved and become a
caramel colour. Draw the pan off the heat and add the water –

take care at this stage as the mixture will boil furiously. Blend the custard powder or cornflour to a thin paste with a little of the milk and add the remainder to the caramel. Return the pan to the heat and stir until the caramel has dissolved and milk is almost boiling. Add a little of the hot milk to the custard, blend and then return all to the milk saucepan and bring up to the boil, stirring all the time. Serve warm sprinkled with the nuts.

Easy lemon soufflé

Serves 4–6

water – see recipe
1 packet lemon jelly
finely grated rind and juice of
  1 lemon

1 large can evaporated milk
125 ml/¼ pint double cream
chopped walnuts for decoration

Measure 125 ml/¼ pint cold water into a saucepan and bring up to the boil. Draw the pan off the heat and add the jelly in pieces. Stir until dissolved – it's not necessary to replace the pan over the heat. Make the dissolved jelly up to 250 ml/½ pint with cold water, using about 3 tablespoons extra water. Add the lemon rind and set aside until cooled and almost beginning to set.

Whisk the evaporated milk – use it from a chilled can if possible – and strained lemon juice together until thick and light. Then gradually whisk in the jelly. Continue to beat until the mixture begins to thicken noticeably, then quickly fold in the cream and pour the mixture into a pretty serving dish. Sprinkle with chopped walnuts and set aside until set quite firm.

Raspberry cream with crunch topping

Serves 4

1 packet vanilla instant pudding
milk – see recipe
1 small packet frozen raspberries

for the crunch topping:
25 g/1 oz butter
2 level tablespoons soft brown
  sugar
15 g/½ oz cornflakes
1 tablespoon finely chopped
  walnuts

Empty the packet of vanilla pudding into a mixing basin. Add the milk according to instructions on the packet – usually 500 ml/1 pint – and stir until beginning to thicken. Stir in the still frozen raspberries – the fruit will thaw while the pudding is chilling. If the fruit is partially or completely thawed it makes no difference. Spoon the mixture into the base of 4 individual serving dishes and allow to set.

Meanwhile melt the butter in a medium-sized saucepan, add the sugar and stir until melted. Stir in the cornflakes and nuts and using a fork, so as not to break up the cornflakes, stir until ingredients are well coated. Draw the pan off the heat and allow to cool, stirring occasionally with the fork to keep the pieces separate. Then sprinkle over pudding tops just before serving – the crunch would go soft if left sitting on the dessert too long beforehand.

Little, quick recipes

Peach crumb whip Cut any left-over cake, frosting and all, into cubes. Add cubed canned peaches, coarsely chopped nuts and fold into lightly whipped cream. Chill if possible before serving.

Orange-baked peaches Combine equal amounts of orange juice and peach syrup with a little grated orange rind, brown sugar, whole cloves and butter. Pour over canned cling peach halves in shallow baking pan. Bake in a moderate oven for 15 minutes. Serve warm with cream.

Rice and raspberries Empty contents of large can creamed rice into basin and fold in 125 ml/¼ pint whipped cream and one packet thawed frozen raspberries. Sweeten if necessary.

Fruit and shortbread fingers To any drained canned fruit syrup, add a little sherry or brandy. Pour over fruit and serve fruit topped with whipped cream. Hand round, separately, shortbread fingers.

Fruit fool Stir 4–5 tablespoons condensed milk into 250 ml/½ pint unsweetened fruit purée (blackcurrant is specially delicious). Serve in individual glass dishes and hand round sponge fingers.

Peach mallow Fill canned peach halves with chopped canned pineapple. Top with snipped marshmallows and put under hot grill until the marshmallows turn golden brown. Serve hot.

Butterscotch crunch Prepare instant butterscotch pudding according to instructions on packet. When it is beginning to set, fold in 125 ml/¼ pint whipped cream. Spoon into serving glasses and top with crushed peanut brittle.

Easy trifle Line a dish with broken sponge fingers and sprinkle with chopped glacé cherries. Pour in prepared instant pudding. When it is set, decorate top with whipped cream and walnuts.

Old-fashioned chocolate pudding Prepare instant chocolate dessert according to instructions on packet. Pour into individual serving dishes and top with brown sugar and finely chopped walnuts. Serve with single cream.

Fruit cream Pour a prepared instant whip over either cut up orange sections or canned pineapple chunks and sliced banana. Chill before serving.

Grape cocktail Halve and de-seed 200 g/8 oz green grapes. Divide equally between 4 serving glasses and sprinkle with sauterne wine or sweet sherry. Top with a spoonful of soured cream and a sprinkling of brown sugar.

Pineapple mallow whip Drain the juice from 1 × 340 g/12 oz can pineapple pieces and combine with 100 g/4 oz snipped marshmallows – use scissors dipped in water to prevent marshmallows sticking. Place in the refrigerator to chill for 1 hour, then fold in 250 ml/½ pint double cream, stiffly whipped.

Rice sundae Drain the contents of 1 × 411 g/14½ can fruit cocktail and spoon alternate layers of fruit and canned creamed rice into individual serving glasses. Top with whipped cream and chopped nuts – for extra flavour add 1 tablespoon brandy to the cream before whipping.

Quick coffee rice Dissolve ½ teaspoon instant coffee in a little hot water and stir in the contents of 1 × 440 g/15½ oz can creamed rice. Spoon into four individual serving dishes and top with whipped cream and chopped walnuts.

Iced white peaches Empty the contents of 1 × 425 g/15 oz can white peaches into pretty serving dish; chill until ready to serve.

Banana tango Slice bananas and cover with canned orange juice.

Pears in port Drain canned pear halves. Pour over sufficient port to cover and chill till ready to serve.

Caramelized pears Sprinkle drained canned pear halves with lemon juice, then with melted butter and a little brown sugar and ground nutmeg or cinnamon. Grill about 8 minutes or until golden. Serve topped with soft vanilla ice cream.

Pineapple sauté Sauté canned pineapple slices or peach halves in butter till golden. Serve topped with ice cream, then with some of the fruit syrup and perhaps a touch of sherry.

Jelly jumble Prepare a fruit jelly and when firm run a fork through it. Heap on canned pineapple or fruit cocktail.

Snow-capped plums Top canned purple plums with a generous spoonful of sour cream and a little grated nutmeg.

Plum medley Combine a can each of purple plums and greengage plums; add a little lemon juice and a pinch of ground mace.

Frosty peaches Top frozen or canned peach slices with this ice cream sauce. Stir 500 ml/1 pint vanilla ice cream until soft, but not runny. Add a few drops almond essence.

Hot peaches Heat canned peaches or fruit cocktail, juice and all, with a little lemon peel. Serve as it is, or on top of vanilla ice cream.

Continental platter Serve fresh oranges or grapes and cheese for dessert.

Frosted strawberries Top thawed frozen sliced strawberries with commercial soured cream, then a sprinkling of brown sugar.

Minute savers

*Beaten egg whites break down if left to stand – so only whip up just before adding to the recipe.

*Eggs separate more easily when cold from the refrigerator, but whites beat up to a better volume when at room temperature.

*Rinse a saucepan with cold water before heating milk or making custards. Makes cleaning afterwards easier.

*Add any flavouring or sugar to double cream *before* whisking up, not afterwards. This reduces the risk of over-beating.

*To make a plain jelly set quickly, dissolve the jelly in half quantity of boiling water. Make up with ice cubes and by the time the cubes have melted the jelly will be almost setting.

*Before squeezing lemons, roll between the hand to warm a little. You'll find the juice will flow more easily.

Quick breads, cakes and pastry

Quick breads raised with baking powder, a new revolutionary easy-mix method for mixing cakes and home-made pastry mixes to store in the refrigerator make it possible for even the busiest of cooks to bake at week-ends.

The term quick bread nearly always applies to fruit breads or easy plain loaves risen using baking powder or a mixture of cream of tartar and bicarbonate of soda. Rich fruity breads keep well but other plainer breads should be eaten quickly.

For simple yeast breads any cook can keep a tin of dried yeast in the store cupboard. Dried yeast is very easy to use and can replace fresh yeast in any recipe. If using dried yeast in a recipe that lists fresh yeast, always use half the quantity of dried yeast, and remember that 1 level tablespoon dried yeast equals 15 g/½ oz or is the equivalent to 25 g/1 oz fresh yeast.

Simple yeast breads and rolls can be made more quickly by proving only once after the dough has been shaped. Although generally accepted that this method does not give as good a texture as the traditional method of proving or rising twice, it's very satisfactory for simple little recipes. When the dough is proved only once, to get a good rise when baking the dough must be very thoroughly kneaded to develop the gluten.

The best kind of tins for baking fruit breads are plain loaf tins in preference to bread tins; they are not so deep and make fruit breads a more attractive shape. When preparing for use, grease well then line with a strip of greased greaseproof paper, cut the width of the pan and long enough to cover the base and two opposite ends of the tin – it's not necessary to line the sides.

Quick plain loaf

Makes 1 loaf
400 g/1 lb self-raising flour
1 level teaspoon salt
250 ml/½ pint milk

Sift the flour and salt into a mixing basin. Using a fork stir in the milk and mix to a rough dough. Turn out on to a lightly floured working surface and knead to a round about 2.5 cm/1 thick.

Place in a baking tray, dredged with flour, in the centre of a moderately hot oven (190°C, 375°F or Gas No. 5) and bake for 30–40 minutes. This bread is best eaten within a day since it gets stale very quickly.

Hot seed rolls

Makes 18
400 g/1 lb self-raising flour
2 level teaspoons baking powder
1 level teaspoon salt
100 g/4 oz butter or margarine
150 ml/ good ⅓ pint milk
milk for brushing
poppy, caraway or sesame seeds

Sift the flour, baking powder and salt into a large mixing basin. Add the fat in pieces and rub into the mixture thoroughly to distribute the fat evenly. Hollow out a well in the dry ingredients and pour all the milk into the centre. Using a fork for easiest handling, blend quickly to a rough dough. Turn on to a lightly floured working surface and knead to a smooth dough; add only enough flour to prevent dough sticking to the table.

Divide the dough into 3 portions and then divide each portion into 6 smaller pieces. With floured hands – this way the dough won't stick to your fingers – roll each piece out to a rope about 15 cm/6 in long.

Tie each of the first six pieces of dough into a simple knot, place on a greased baking tray, brush with milk and sprinkle with poppy seeds.

Roll the next six into whorls; starting at one end, simply roll the rope of dough back along itself. Lay flat on a greased baking tray, brush with milk and sprinkle with sesame seeds.

Shape the last six pieces of dough into loops. Turn each end into the centre and then draw ends up together. Lay flat on a greased baking tray, brush with milk and sprinkle with caraway seeds.

Place above centre in a very hot oven (220°C, 425°F or Gas No. 7) and bake for 15 minutes until browned. If rolls are on two trays, place on a lower shelf, moving up to the top when first tray is baked, for further 5 minutes browning. Nicest served warm.

Milk bread

Makes 1 loaf

200 g/8 oz plain white flour
1 level teaspoon salt
1 level teaspoon castor sugar
125 ml/¼ pint milk and water mixed

2 level teaspoons dried yeast
25 g/1 oz butter or margarine
milk
poppy or caraway seeds

First lift the flour and salt into a warm mixing basin and set aside in a warm place while gathering together the remaining ingredients.

Dissolve the sugar in the lukewarm liquid and sprinkle over the dried yeast. Leave until frothy – this takes about 10 minutes. Rub butter or margarine into the warmed flour and stir in the yeasty liquid. Mix to a dough and beat by hand for about 5 minutes.

Turn on to a lightly floured surface and knead a further 5 minutes to improve the texture. Divide the dough into three pieces and roll each into a strand, about 25–30 cm/10–12 in long. Press three ends together (use a small weight to hold in place) and plait into a loaf. Nip the ends together to join and place on a greased baking tray. Put all this aside in a greased polythene bag. Set in a warm place until loaf has risen and doubled in size – 15–20 minutes.

Brush with a little milk and sprinkle with poppy or caraway seeds if liked. Place near the top of a very hot oven (230°C, 450°F or Gas No. 8) and bake for 5 or 10 minutes. Lower heat to moderately hot (190°C, 375° F or Gas No. 5) and bake for a further 10–15 minutes.

Cheese bread

Makes 1 large loaf

400 g/1 lb self-raising flour
pinch of salt and cayenne pepper
100 g/4 oz margarine

150 g/6 oz Cheddar cheese, grated
2 eggs, made up to 250 ml/½ pint with milk

Sieve the flour, salt and cayenne pepper. Rub in the margarine and add the cheese. Stir the eggs and milk mixture into the other ingredients, using a fork to mix to a soft dough.

Turn out on to a lightly floured working surface, shape neatly and place in a buttered large loaf tin.

Place in the centre of a moderately hot oven (190°C, 375°F or Gas No. 5) and bake for 1 hour. Allow to cool, then serve sliced – delicious toasted.

Soft bread rolls

Makes 18

400 g/1 lb plain flour
2 level teaspoons salt
125 ml/¼ pint milk
2 tablespoons salad oil
1 level tablespoon dried yeast

125 ml/¼ pint warm water
1 level teaspoon castor sugar
butter or oil for glazing
caraway, poppy or celery seeds

Sift together the flour and salt into a medium-sized mixing basin. Mix together the milk and oil and set aside. Sprinkle the dried yeast on top of the mixed water and sugar and stand in a warm place for 10 minutes until frothy.

Make a well in the centre of the flour and add the milk, oil and yeast liquid, and using a knife mix to a soft dough, adding more flour if necessary. Turn out on to a lightly floured working surface and knead well for 5 minutes. Divide the dough into 18 equal-sized pieces and roll each piece into a smooth round roll and place ¼ in apart on greased baking tray. Stand in a warm place until well risen. Brush with melted butter or oil, sprinkle with seeds if liked and place in the centre of a hot oven (220°C, 425°F or Gas No. 7) and bake for 20 minutes, or until pale golden brown. Remove from the oven and allow to cool. Pull buns apart and serve warm with butter.

The dough may be placed in the refrigerator overnight, after it has been shaped, but it must be allowed to warm to room temperature before baking.

Irish soda bread (plain)

Makes 1 loaf

400 g/1 lb plain flour
½ level teaspoon bicarbonate of
 soda
½ level teaspoon salt

250 ml/½ pint sour milk or fresh
 milk soured with 2 teaspoons
 lemon juice

Sieve the flour, soda and salt into a bowl. Make a well in the centre and pour in all the milk. To sour fresh milk, add lemon juice and stand in warm place 5 minutes. Using a fork mix to a rough dough in the basin, then turn out on to a working surface and knead until firm – about 3 turns. Turn smooth side up, flatten with the hand a little and place on a lightly floured baking tray. Cut a cross using a sharp knife in the centre of the bread almost through to the base, cutting the bread into 4 portions.

Place above centre in a hot oven (220°C, 425°F or Gas No. 7) and bake for 25–35 minutes or until done. To test if cooked, turn and tap – if there is a hollow sound, it's done. Place on a wire cooling tray; if a soft crust is preferred, wrap in a damp glass cloth.

Variation

Irish soda bread (sweet)

400 g/1 lb plain flour
½ level teaspoon bicarbonate of
 soda
1 level teaspoon salt
25 g/1 oz butter

100 g/4 oz cleaned currants
1 teaspoon castor sugar
250 ml/½ pint sour milk or fresh
 milk soured with 2 teaspoons
 lemon juice

Proceed as above, then rub in the butter to the sieved ingredients. Add the currants, sugar and soured milk. Mix and knead to a dough, mark and bake as above.

Fruit tea bread

Makes 1 large loaf

250 g/10 oz mixed sultanas and
  seedless raisins
175 g/7 oz soft brown sugar
250 ml/½ pint cold tea without
  milk

1 large egg
250 g/10 oz self-raising flour (or
  use self-raising wholemeal flour,
  usually to be found at health
  food stores)

Measure the sultanas, raisins and brown sugar into a bowl. Pour
over the cold tea and leave overnight. The dried fruit will soak
up the tea to become plump and juicy, making a deliciously moist
loaf.

Next day stir the ingredients once or twice, then lightly mix
the egg and add with the flour. Using a wooden spoon mix well
until smooth. Pour into a well-greased 1 kg/2 lb loaf tin which
has been lined with a strip of greaseproof paper cut to cover the
base and overlap the two ends. Spread the mixture level. Bake
in the centre of a moderate oven (180°C, 350°F, Gas Mark 4) for
1½ hours.

Yorkshire bun loaf

Makes 1 large loaf

250 g/10 oz self-raising flour
½ level teaspoon salt
100 g/4 oz butter or margarine
75 g/3 oz castor sugar
75 g/3 oz sultanas

2 large eggs
1 dessertspoon marmalade (chop
  up any large pieces)
1–2 tablespoons milk

Sift the flour and salt into a mixing basin. Add the butter or
margarine in slices and rub into the mixture. Add the sugar and
dried fruit. Lightly mix together the eggs and marmalade and,
using a fork, stir into the mixture along with sufficient milk to
mix to a stiff dough.

Spoon the dough into a greased 1 kg/2 lb loaf tin, spread
evenly, hollowing out the centre slightly. Place in the centre of
a moderately hot oven (190°C, 375°F or Gas No. 5) and bake for
1 hour. Allow to cool in the tin, then serve sliced with butter.

Easy-mix cakes

Using a quick one-stage mix, the ingredients for the cake are blended thoroughly for one minute only and the mixture is ready for baking. It's a brand new idea and has proved a very successful one. *This method cannot be used for any cake recipe* since proportions for one-stage cakes are carefully worked out. For instance, most recipes use self-raising flour with added baking powder – this gives extra rise, since, without the long creaming process normally used, less air is incorporated.

All ingredients must be at room temperature; this applies particularly to the margarine, eggs and milk – and it's important that none of these are used straight from the refrigerator. Quick creaming margarines are most satisfactory, the fat blending in evenly with remaining ingredients – *never use butter* which, although ideal in normal cake recipes is too hard a fat for one-stage cakes.

Swiss roll

Makes 8–10 slices

100 g/4 oz self-raising flour
1 level teaspoon baking powder
100 g/4 oz castor sugar
100 g/4 oz quick creaming
 margarine

2 large eggs
little castor sugar
250 ml/½ pint double cream
 little icing sugar

Sift the flour and baking powder into a large mixing basin. Add the sugar, margarine, cut in slices, and eggs. Mix thoroughly and then beat with a wooden spoon for 1 minute.

Spoon the mixture into a greased and lined Swiss roll tin. Spread the mixture evenly – particularly in the corners of the tin. Place in the centre of a moderately hot oven (190°C, 375°F or Gas No. 5) and bake for 15–20 minutes or until evenly risen and brown.

Immediately the Swiss roll is baked turn out on to a sheet of greaseproof paper, previously sprinkled with castor sugar. Using a knife trim away the edges and roll up, leaving the paper inside. Leave to cool.

Whip the cream until thick, then finish the Swiss roll; very gently unroll, only enough to remove the greaseproof paper. Using a knife, spread the cream over the inside of the sponge and quickly re-roll again. Sprinkle with icing sugar and cut in slices.

Family fruit cake

Makes one 15 cm/6 in cake

200 g/8 oz self-raising flour
1 rounded teaspoon mixed spice
100 g/4 oz castor sugar
100 g/4 oz quick creaming
 margarine

150 g/6 oz mixed dried fruit
50 g/2 oz cherries, rinsed and
 halved
2 large eggs
2 tablespoons milk

Sift the flour and mixed spice into a large mixing bowl. Add all the remaining ingredients, slicing up the margarine. Mix thoroughly then beat with a wooden spoon for 1 minute.

Spoon the mixture into a greased and lined 15 cm/6 in round cake tin. Smooth the top of the mixture. Place in the centre of a slow oven (160°C, 325°F or Gas No. 3) and bake for 1½–2 hours. A warm skewer gently pushed into the centre of the cake should come out clean. Allow baked cake to cool before removing from tin.

Mocha gâteau

Makes one 17.5 cm/7 in cake

125 g/5 oz self-raising flour
pinch salt
pinch bicarbonate of soda
1 level teaspoon baking powder
25 g/1 oz cocoa powder
100 g/4 oz castor sugar
100 g/4 oz quick creaming
 margarine

1 level tablespoon golden syrup
2 eggs
3 tablespoons milk
1 teaspoon coffee essence
coffee butter cream – see recipe
 on page 173
little icing sugar

Sift carefully the flour, salt, bicarbonate of soda, baking powder and cocoa powder together into a large mixing basin. Add all remaining ingredients, slicing up the margarine. Mix together thoroughly and then using a wooden spoon beat well for 1 minute. Divide the mixture equally between two greased and lined 17.5 cm/7 in sandwich tins. Spread the mixture level and place in the centre of a moderate oven (180°C, 350°F or Gas No. 4) and bake for 20–25 minutes.

Cool and then sandwich with coffee butter cream. Dust with sifted icing sugar.

Cherry cake

Makes one 17.5 cm/7 inch cake

200 g/8 oz self-raising flour
2 level teaspoons baking powder
½ level teaspoon salt
100 g/4 oz glacé cherries, rinsed and quartered

100 g/4 oz quick creaming margarine
100 g/4 oz castor sugar
2 large eggs
½ teaspoon vanilla essence
2 tablespoons milk

Sift together the flour, baking powder and salt into a large mixing basin. Pat cherries dry and mix into the flour. Add all the remaining ingredients, slicing up the margarine. Mix thoroughly then beat with a wooden spoon for 1 minute. Spoon the mixture into a greased and lined 17.5 cm/7 in round cake tin. Spread the mixture level and hollow out the centre slightly. Place in the centre of a moderate oven (180°C, 350°F or Gas No. 4) and bake for 1 hour or until risen and firm.

Cinnamon spice cake

Makes one 17.5 cm/7 in cake

100 g/4 oz self-raising flour
1 rounded teaspoon cinnamon
1 level teaspoon baking powder
100 g/4 oz castor sugar
100 g/4 oz quick creaming margarine
2 eggs
little icing sugar

for the filling:

100 g/4 oz icing sugar
1 rounded teaspoon cinnamon
50 g/2 oz quick creaming margarine
1 dessertspoon milk

Sift the flour, cinnamon and baking powder into a large mixing bowl. Add the sugar, margarine, cut in slices, and eggs. Mix thoroughly and then beat with a wooden spoon for 1 minute.

Dividing the mixture evenly, spoon into 2 greased and lined 17.5 cm/7 in sponge cake tins. Smooth tops, hollowing out in the centre slightly. Place in the centre of a moderate oven (180°C, 350°F or Gas No. 4). Allow to cool before filling.

Sieve the icing sugar and cinnamon into a small mixing basin. Add the margarine and milk and then beat together until thoroughly mixed. Sandwich the two layer cakes with the filling and dust the top with a little sieved icing sugar.

Christmas or birthday fruit cake

Makes one 20 cm/8 in cake

400 g/1 lb self-raising flour
2 rounded teaspoons mixed spice
200 g/8 oz castor sugar
200 g/8 oz quick creaming
  margarine
100 g/6 oz currants
150 g/6 oz sultanas

100 g/4 oz cherries, rinsed and
  halved
4 large eggs
4 tablespoons of milk or 2
  tablespoons of milk and
  2 tablespoons of brandy

Sift the flour and mixed spice into a large mixing bowl. Add all the remaining ingredients, slicing up the margarine. Mix thoroughly then beat with a wooden spoon for one minute.

Spoon into a greased and lined 20 cm/8 in round deep cake tin. Place in the centre of a slow oven (160°C, 325°F or Gas No. 3) and bake for 1½ hours, then lower the heat to cool (150°C, 300°F or Gas No. 2) and bake for a further hour.

A warm skewer gently pushed into the centre of the cake should come out clean. Allow to cool before removing from the tin.

Cream sponge sandwich

Makes one 17.5 cm/7 in cake

100 g/4 oz self-raising flour
1 level teaspoon baking powder
100 g/4 oz castor sugar
100 g/4 oz quick creaming
  margarine
2 large eggs
vanilla essence
2 tablespoons raspberry jam
little sieved icing sugar

for the filling

50 g/2 oz quick creaming
  margarine
50 g/2 oz castor sugar
6 teaspoons hot water
4 teaspoons cold milk

First prepare the sponge layers. Sift the flour and baking powder into a large mixing basin. Add the sugar, margarine, cut in slices, eggs and a few drops of vanilla essence. Mix the ingredients thoroughly and beat with a wooden spoon for 1 minute.

Dividing the mixture evenly, spoon into two greased and lined 17.5 cm/7 inch sponge cake tins. Place in the centre of a moderate oven (180°C, 350°F or Gas No. 4) and bake for 25–30 minutes or until risen and firm to the touch. Remove from the tins and allow to cool.

For the filling – cream together the sugar and margarine until light. Beat in the hot water one teaspoon at a time. At this stage the mixture will be very soft. Gradually add the milk, beating very thoroughly between each addition.

To finish the cake when cool, spread the base of one sponge layer with the raspberry jam. Spoon on cream filling and cover jam. Top with remaining sponge layer; dust with icing sugar.

Variation

Orange cup cakes Use finely grated rind of 1 orange instead of vanilla essence and make as above. Spoon into 18 small paper baking cases. Bake near top of a fairly hot oven (200°C, 400°F or Gas No. 6) for 15–20 minutes, or until risen and brown. Allow to cool. Top with orange glacé icing made with 200 g/8 oz icing sugar and enough orange juice to blend to a smooth coating consistency (see recipe on page 173) for glacé icing). Decorate with crystallized orange slices or pieces of angelica.

Frosted coconut cake

Makes one 17.5 cm/7 in cake

125 g/5 oz self-raising flour	2 tablespoons milk
1½ level teaspoons baking powder	¼ teaspoon vanilla essence
40 g/1½ oz desiccated coconut	vanilla butter cream – see recipe
100 g/4 oz castor sugar	on page 172
100 g/4 oz quick creaming	vanilla glacé icing – see page 173
margarine	desiccated coconut for decoration
2 large eggs	

Sift the flour and baking powder into a large mixing basin. Add all the remaining ingredients, slicing up the margarine. Mix thoroughly then beat with a wooden spoon for 1 minute. Dividing the mixture equally, spoon into 2 greased and lined shallow 17.5 cm/7 in sponge cake tins. Place in the centre of a moderately hot oven (190°C, 375°F or Gas No. 5) and bake for 20–25 minutes, or until risen and firm to the touch.

To finish the cake, sandwich with vanilla-flavoured butter cream, coloured a delicate pink. Coat the top with the palest pink vanilla glacé icing and sprinkle with desiccated coconut, whilst the icing is still wet.

Rich chocolate cake

Makes one 17.5 cm/7 in cake
100 g/4 oz self-raising flour
1 level teaspoon baking powder
1 heaped tablespoon cocoa
  powder
100 g/4 oz castor sugar
100 g/4 oz quick creaming
  margarine
2 large eggs
1 tablespoon milk

for the coffee cream icing:
150 g/6 oz icing sugar
100 g/4 oz quick creaming
  margarine
3 teaspoons coffee essence

Sift the flour, baking powder and cocoa powder into a large mixing basin. Add all the remaining ingredients, slicing up the margarine. Mix thoroughly then beat with a wooden spoon for 1 minute.

Dividing the mixture evenly, spoon into two greased and lined 17.5 cm/7 inch sponge cake tins. Place in the centre of a moderate oven (180°C, 350°F or Gas No. 4) and bake for 25–30 minutes or until risen and firm to the touch. Cool on a cake rack.

Sieve the icing sugar into a small mixing basin. Add the margarine and coffee essence. Beat thoroughly until smooth and creamy. Sandwich the cooled cakes with half the icing. Spoon the remainder on to the top of the cake and spread evenly. Use the tip of a teaspoon to rough up the icing to a pretty design.

Fillings and icings

Quick vanilla butter cream

To fill and top one 17.5 cm–20 cm/7–8 in sponge cake
75 g/3 oz quick creaming
  margarine
200 g/8 oz icing sugar

2 dessertspoons milk
½ teaspoon vanilla essence
colouring (optional)

Place all the ingredients in a mixing basin and beat together with a wooden spoon until well mixed – takes 2–3 minutes. Add colouring if required.

Variations

Chocolate butter cream Blend 1 heaped tablespoon cocoa with 2 tablespoons hot water and cool. Omit milk in the recipe and use this chocolate mixture.

Coffee butter cream Replace 1 dessertspoon milk with 1 dessert-spoon coffee essence.

Orange butter cream Use 2 dessertspoons orange juice plus a little colouring.

Lemon butter cream Use 2 dessertspoons lemon juice plus a little colouring.

Lemon filling

To fill one 17.5–20 cm/7–8 in cake
125 ml/¼ pint double cream
4 tablespoons lemon curd

Whip the cream until stiff and then fold in the lemon curd. Use as a filling for sponge cake layers.

Vanilla glacé icing

To cover top and sides of two 17.5–
  20 cm 7–8 in cakes
200 g/8 oz icing sugar
2–3 tablespoons hot water
few drops vanilla essence
colouring (if required)

Sieve the icing sugar into a mixing basin. Stir in the hot water – this makes the icing set up more quickly – and the vanilla essence. Add a few drops of colouring if required for a particular recipe. Pour immediately over the top of the cake and using a knife spread evenly over top and sides.

Chocolate cream icing

To fill and top two 17.5–20 cm/7–8 in sponge cakes

1 × 113 g/4 oz packet chocolate chips
pinch salt

1 × 142 ml/5 fl oz carton soured cream

Empty the chocolate pieces into a mixing basin and set over a pan half filled with hot, not boiling, water. Stir until chocolate is melted and smooth, then remove from the heat. Stir in a pinch of salt and the soured cream. Blend until smooth then use as required; this frosting sets firm on cooling.

Chocolate fudge frosting

To top two 17.5 cm/7 in sponge cakes

100 g/4 oz plain chocolate
2 tablespoons water
15 g/½ oz butter or margarine

few drops vanilla essence
100 g/4 oz sieved icing sugar

Measure the chocolate, water and butter into a small saucepan and heat very slowly over a very low heat, until smooth and blended. Draw the pan off the heat and stir in vanilla essence, and then stir in the icing sugar. Allow the icing to cool and become fudgy before using.

Make your own ready-mix for pastry, scones or cakes

Cut out the long job of rubbing fat into flour every time pastry, scones or plain cakes are baked by preparing some of your own ready-mixes. They are very convenient to use as you just weigh out a quantity and add liquid. Store the dry rubbed-in mixtures in closed polythene bags, plastic containers with airtight lids or screw-topped jars, each clearly labelled and dated. They will keep for up to 3 months in a refrigerator.

Just remember that pastry and cake mixes have half as much fat as flour. In a recipe calling for 200 g/8 oz flour and 100 g/4 oz fat, use 300 g/12 oz mix.

For pastry, allow about 1 teaspoon of water for every 40 g/1½ oz mix. Use 150 g/6 oz pastry to cover 750 ml/1½ pint pie dish or line 17.5 cm/7 inch flan ring. Use 225 g/9 oz pastry mix to cover 1.25 litre/2½ pint pie dish, to line 20 cm/8 in flan ring, or to make 8–12 tarts, cut with a 7.5 cm/2½ in cutter. Use 300 g/12 oz pastry mix for a pie with top and bottom pastry. The mixes can be used straight from the refrigerator.

Pastry mix

1.2 kg/3 lb plain flour
3 level teaspoons salt
300 g/12 oz white cooking fat or
 lard
300 g/12 oz margarine

Sift flour and salt. Rub in fats with fingertips until mixture resembles fine breadcrumbs. Store in a closed polythene bag, plastic container with an air-tight lid or a screw-topped jar in a refrigerator or cool dark place.

Shortcrust pastry	To 300 g/12 oz mix, add about 2–3 tablespoons cold water.
Sweet shortcrust	To 300 g/12 oz mix add 1 tablespoon of castor sugar, 1 beaten egg and about 1 tablespoon cold water.
Savoury crumble topping	To 150 g/6 oz mix add ¼ teaspoon mixed herbs and 2–3 tablespoons cold water. Use to cover meat or fish casseroles. Enough for a 750 ml–1 litre/1½–2 pint dish.
Cheese pastry	To 300 g/12 oz mix, add ½ teaspoon dry mustard, pinch cayenne pepper, 50 g/2 oz finely grated cheese and 2–3 tablespoons cold water.

Scone mix

1.2 kg/3 lb self-raising flour
3 level teaspoons salt
400 g/1 lb margarine

Sift the flour and salt. Rub in the margarine until mixture resembles fine breadcrumbs. Store in a closed polythene bag, plastic container with an air-tight lid or screw-topped jar in a refrigerator or cool dark place.

Sweet scones   To 300 g/12 oz mix add 25 g/1 oz castor sugar and about 125 ml/¼ pint milk. Bake at 220°C, 425°F or Gas No. 7 for about 10 minutes.

Cheese scones   To 300 g/12 oz mix add 75 g/3 oz grated cheese and about 125 ml/¼ pint milk. Bake at 220°C, 425°F or Gas No. 7 for about 10 minutes.

Cake mix

1.2 kg/3 lb self-raising flour
3 level teaspoons salt
600 g/1½ lb margarine

Sift flour and salt. Rub in margarine with finger tips until mixture resembles fine breadcrumbs. Store in a closed polythene bag, plastic container with an air-tight lid or a screw-topped jar in a refrigerator or cool dark place.

Apricot buns   To 250 g/10 oz mix add 50 g/2 oz castor sugar, 1 beaten egg, 1 dessertspoon milk, and mix to a stiff dough. Put a dessertspoon of mixture into each bun tin, make a hole in the centre with a spoon handle and drop in a little apricot jam. Bake at 200°C, 400°F or Gas No. 6 for 15–20 minutes. Makes 12.

Fruit cake

To 300 g/12 oz mix add 100 g/4 oz castor sugar, 100 g/4 oz mixed fruit, 2 beaten eggs and 2–3 tablespoons milk. Mix to a stiff dropping consistency. Bake in a lined and greased 15 cm/6 in cake tin at 160°C, 325°F or Gas No. 3 for 1½ hours.

Spiced currant biscuits

To 150 g/6 oz mix add 25 g/1 oz castor sugar, 1 teaspoon cinnamon, 50 g/2 oz currants, 1 egg yolk and 2 teaspoons milk. Work together, then knead until smooth. Roll out to 20 cm/8 in circle, 5 mm/¼ in thick. Cut into 12 triangles. Bake at 180°C, 350°F or Gas No. 4 for 30 minutes.

Currant cakes

Weigh out 300 g/12 oz of the mix. Stir in 75 g/3 oz castor sugar, 75 g/3 oz currants and mix to a soft dropping consistency with 1 egg lightly mixed with 5–6 tablespoons milk. Spoon into 24 paper cases placed in bun tins and bake above centre at 190°C, 375°F or Gas No. 5 for 25–30 minutes, until golden brown and springy to the touch.

Orange cakes

Omit fruit from recipe above; add ½ teaspoon vanilla essence, grated rind of 1 orange and ¼ teaspoon orange essence; ice when cooled with glacé icing made with the orange juice.

Cherry cakes

Proceed as for orange cakes; add ¼ level teaspoon cream of tartar and 50 g/2 oz rinsed and cut glacé cherries.

Rock cakes

Weigh out 150 g/6 oz of the mix. Stir in pinch mixed spice, 40 g/1½ oz castor sugar and 40 g/1½ oz mixed dried fruit. Stir in 1 small egg to mix. Fork in rough heaps on a baking tray and bake just above centre in a hot oven (200°C, 400°F or Gas No. 6) for 15–20 minutes until lightly browned.

Shortbread crumble topping   To 150 g/6 oz mix rub in 50 g/2 oz castor sugar. Use to cover fruit in a 750 ml–1 litre/1½–2 pint pie dish.

Easy-crumb crust for dessert pies

For one 20 cm/8 in pie
1 × 225 g/8 oz packet digestive
  biscuits or ginger snaps
50 g/2 oz butter
1 dessertspoon golden syrup

Crush the biscuits with a rolling pin to make fine crumbs, and set aside. Melt the butter and syrup in a small saucepan over low heat then draw the pan off the heat and using a fork, stir in the crushed biscuit crumbs.

Mix well then spoon all the mixture into the centre of a 20 cm/8 in pie plate. Using the back of the spoon press the mixture over the base and around the sides of the plate and neaten the edges. Set aside to chill while preparing the filling – see recipes that follow.

Spoon filling into the pie shell then place in the refrigerator to chill for several hours. Just before serving, wrap a hot wet towel under the bottom and around the sides of the pie plate. Hold towel against plate for a few minutes to loosen the crust, then slice and serve.

Here are four fruit fillings, each entirely different, which are particularly delicious with this biscuit crumb crust:

Filling variations

Orange mousse filling

Serves 4

250 ml/½ pint water
1 packet orange jelly
juice of 1 orange
1 teaspoon lemon juice

2 × 75 g/3 oz full fat soft cheese
  packets
25 g/1 oz castor sugar

Measure 125 ml/¼ pint of the water into a saucepan and bring up to the boil. Draw the pan off the heat and add the jelly in pieces. Stir until dissolved then stir in the remaining cold water and strained orange and lemon juice.

In a mixing basin cream together the cream cheese and sugar until softened then slowly stirring to blend thoroughly, add the jelly.

Set aside until cool and beginning to thicken, then whisk using a rotary beater until thick and light. Pour into the prepared crumb shell and chill until quite firm before serving.

Lemon cream filling

Serves 6

1 small can condensed milk
125 ml/¼ pint double cream
1 large or 2 small lemons

100 g/4 oz black grapes for
  decoration

Measure the condensed milk and the cream into a mixing basin, finely grate 1 of the lemons, or half if only 1 large lemon is being used, and add to the mixture.

Use the finest side of your grater; remember only the fine yellow zest has the lemon flavour, the white pith underneath is bitter and should not be included. Squeeze the juice from both lemons, strain and add to the mixture. The addition of lemon juice will make the mixture go quite thick after a few minutes stirring.

Pour the lemon mixture into the base of a chilled crumb crust and spread evenly. Decorate around the edges with the halved, de-seeded black grapes and chill before serving.

Peach parfait filling

Serves 4–6

1 × 425 g/15 oz can peach slices
15 g/½ oz powdered gelatine
2 tablespoons lemon juice
25 g/1 oz castor sugar

1 family-size block vanilla ice
  cream
chopped walnuts for decoration

Drain the peaches from the can and set aside. Measure 250 ml/
½ pint of the syrup from the can, making it up with water if
necessary.

In a saucepan sprinkle the gelatine over the lemon juice and
leave to soak for 5 minutes. Add the peach syrup and heat gently,
stirring until dissolved. Draw the pan off the heat, stir in the
sugar and set aside until the sides of the pan can be comfortably
held with the hand – take care not to allow the mixture to become
too cold.

Add the ice cream in lumps to the peach syrup and whisk until
blended, fluffy and beginning to thicken. Reserving a few peach
slices for decoration, quickly fold in remainder and pour into the
prepared crumb shell.

Decorate with reserved peach slices, sprinkle with chopped
nuts and set aside to chill before serving.

Minute savers

*Mark margarine or cooking fat packets into 25 g/1 oz sections
before using. This way you can cut off the exact amount each
time without measuring or guessing.

*Always wash floury pastry boards and rolling pins in cold water
first – hot water makes the flour stick.

*To encourage a bread dough to rise more quickly, place the tin
or bowl of dough inside a large polythene bag and close. Then
set in a warm place – the dampness and warmth kept inside
speeds up rising.

*Use lightly floured hands to shape scone or bread doughs; this
helps prevent the mixture sticking to your fingers.

*Measure out ingredients and pre-heat the oven before starting on quick-mix cake or bread recipes – those with raising agent added should be mixed quickly and put in the oven immediately for best results.

*Keep lots of ready-cut paper liners for tins in a kitchen drawer. It's easy to cut out several at one time and less wasteful, too.

The professional touch

A clever cook always presents her food looking pretty and appetizing. However simple the recipe may be, the use of herbs and seasonings or a pretty garnish all help to make food more interesting.

Quick short-cut cooking depends on this kind of imagination more than anything else; a subtle flavour and an attractive appearance make all the difference and are the marks of a clever, interested cook.

How to prepare a pretty garnish

Parsley
Choose bright green parsley with tight curly leaves. Nip the curly heads off the stalks, wash in cold water and shake or pat dry in a tea towel. Curly tops may be snipped off and used as a garnish simply as sprigs, or sprigs may be chopped. Collect in a small bunch, place on a chopping board and use a sharp medium-sized kitchen knife – without a serrated edge. To chop parsley correctly, use the heel of the knife, as opposed to the tip. Using the left hand, push the parsley under the heel of the knife while chopping with the right hand – this cuts the parsley coarsely.

For further fine chopping, hold the tip of the knife with the fingers of the left hand, keeping the tip of the knife on the board and chop using the right hand, swinging the knife back and forwards over the parsley, chopping until fine enough. Parsley is best stored unchopped if kept for any length of time (see page 17)

To use: Parsley sprigs look pretty tucked in between stacks of sandwiches, placed on the top of shellfish cocktails, decorating open sandwiches or prepared meat dishes. Sprinkle chopped parsley over scrambled egg, buttered vegetables, especially carrots and new potatoes, or vegetables in a white sauce such as onions, cauliflowers or leeks. Sprinkle over fried fish, or over mixed grills, pork or lamb chops. Looks pretty on potato salad or simple hors d'oeuvre, such as sardines, tomato slices or hard-boiled eggs.

Tomato

Choose firm, ripe tomatoes. Unripe tomatoes are difficult to peel; soft ones are difficult to cut. Skins from tomatoes may be removed if liked before using. Simply nick the skins of the tomatoes with a sharp knife on the rounded side, plunge into boiling water for 1 minute and then drain. Peel off the skins – where the tomato was nicked the skin will already have begun to curl up.

Tomato slices make a simple and effective decoration. Slice tomatoes cleanly either using a very sharp steel kitchen knife or a serrated knife such as a bread knife. Place tomato stalk end to the table surface and slice downwards. Keep slices in correct order so they retain the tomato shape and lay flat. Alternatively, tomatoes may first be cut in half, then into quarters. Dip centre edge in finely grated Parmesan cheese, or finely chopped parsley.

Tomatoe lilies are cut using a small, sharp pointed kitchen knife. Hold the tomato in the left hand and with the knife in the right hand push the knife up into the centre of the tomato at an angle. Work around the centre of the tomato placing the knife at opposite angles for each cut, taking care to hit the tomato centre each time. When completed, lift the two halves apart and place a small sprig of parsley in each centre.

To use: Sliced tomatoes look marvellous on open sandwiches, decorating grilled hamburgers, over potato topping on shepherd's pie and on baked or grilled fish. Cut into wedges or tomato lilies to decorate salads, plates of sandwiches or garnish cold meats.

Cucumber

Cucumber can be peeled or left unpeeled and then sliced at an angle. Garnish slices with a thin slice of stuffed olive or a sprig of parsley in the centre. Try alternating slices of cucumber and tomato in a row and decorate with chopped parsley. Try placing

cucumber slices over a slice of lemon, cut through both with a sharp knife from outer edge to the centre only. Turn edges inwards, overlapping to make a cone, and place a sprig of parsley in the cone. Or, twist edges in opposite directions to make a cucumber and lemon twist.

Keep cucumber stalk end downwards in a glass of water – cover cut end with kitchen foil.

To Use: Cucumber slices look fresh and crisp over cold fish or served with cold meats or ham. Arrange cones on open sandwiches, or around the edge of any plate along with snipped cress. Cucumber and lemon twists look dramatic on crab or lobster salad, or fried fish dishes.

Lemon
Lemons are ideal for garnishes and are very versatile. They may be cut across making pretty lemon slices – garnish centre with sliced stuffed olive or chopped parsley. Or cut the lemon lengthwise into wedges and dip lemon centre edge in chopped parsley or paprika.

A lemon left plain may be sliced to make lemon butterflies. Cut plain slices in half, then cut each half to the centre into quarters but leave the centre segments attached. Gently open out and garnish with parsley sprigs. Lemon twists can be made cutting plain lemon slices into the centre then twist the two edges in opposite directions, add a sprig of parsley if liked.

Remember when cutting lemons to use a stainless steel knife as the acid in the fruit discolours steel knives and the lemon flesh, unless wiped between each slice.

To Use: Lemon goes best with fish dishes. Garnish fried fish with lemon butterflies or slices adding a little chopped parsley. Fix lemon slices on rims of glasses with shellfish cocktail. Serve lemon twists with veal or pork escalopes or veal blanquette or decorate shrimp or prawn open sandwiches. Lemon wedges go with potted prawns, smoked fish, or pancakes.

Paprika pepper

Paprika pepper is a bright red colour and used in cookery mostly for the colour that it contributes. It should not be confused with cayenne pepper which is also bright red but has a very hot and pungent flavour.

The use of paprika pepper is limited; attractive lines of paprika pepper can be used as a garnish on egg slices or lemon wedges. Tip pepper out on to a square of kitchen foil or greaseproof paper. Then using a knife pick up evenly along the knife edge as much pepper as you wish to use in the decoration. Tip quickly over the items to be garnished making a straight even line. This procedure can be used with very finely chopped parsley and the two used together give a pretty contrast in colour. Pinches of paprika pepper are pretty for adding a colour contrast in otherwise plain food.

Paprika pepper comes in jars with shaker tops – store in a cool dry cupboard; once you buy a bottle it will last for months.

To use: It makes a nice colour contrast sprinkled over vegetables in white sauce particularly cauliflower, or scrambled eggs, or over a creamy potato salad along with snipped chives. Lines of paprika look dramatic across egg mayonnaise.

Nuts

Jars of nuts are invaluable for dessert decorations. Walnuts and almonds are the most useful. Walnuts may be used whole or chopped. Coarsely chop walnuts, using scissors, and snip them into pieces. For finely chopped walnuts, chop them in the same

manner as parsley. Never mince walnuts; the pressure squeezes out nut oils and the fine pieces stick together.

Almonds may be purchased in their skins, blanched or chopped; or as almond nibs or flakes – finely sliced. To blanch almonds, that is to remove the outer brown skin on whole almonds, plunge the almonds into boiling water for 1 minute. Drain and quickly pop the almonds out of the skins. While almonds are still warm, it's a good idea to chop or slice them. When cold and hardened they tend to break up more. Toasted almonds have a delicious flavour and look prettier than the untoasted ones. Spread almonds out on a baking tray or grill pan under high heat. Either way shake the almonds occasionally to get even colouring and don't leave them – they burn very quickly.

To Use: Chopped walnuts are nice sprinkled over any custard-based desserts, and over instant whips or ice cream. Flaked toasted almonds are delicious over creamed rice desserts, canned pears, specially nice with apricots, old-fashioned chocolate pudding, blancmange or apple snow.

Coconut

Desiccated coconut being plain white lends itself ideally to added colouring for decoration. Spoon the required amount into a jar; unless specially required, don't do more than 2 tablespoons at a time. Add a few drops of any colouring – best to use are red, green or yellow. Cover with a lid, cap or piece of kitchen foil and shake vigorously to colour all the coconut evenly. Tip the coconut out on to a square of foil and leave in a warm place to dry – before storing in the jar.

Toasted coconut is also effective; spread coconut over a square of kitchen foil in base of a grill pan and toast, under high heat, shaking until evenly browned.

To Use: Sprinkle over whipped cream toppings, particularly round edges of trifles or moulded milk puddings.

Chocolate

Plain chocolate is more suitable than milk chocolate, the darker colour being more effective as a colour contrast. To get more striking shapes and texture, chocolate should be melted and then used. Break the chocolate into a small mixing basin and set this over a pan of hot water – take care to select a basin that fits the pan neatly.

Heat the water in the pan until almost boiling, and draw off the heat, before setting in the basin. Chocolate should *never be melted over direct heat*, nor should any water, even in the form of steam from the pan, be allowed to come in contact with it. Chocolate has unusual properties, and its texture and shiny appearance can easily be spoiled. When melted, spread the chocolate on to a flat surface.

For chocolate rolls, spread the chocolate thinly on marble or Formica and allow to cool but not set firm. Then choose a medium-to-large kitchen knife with a plain edge. Holding the knife tipped backwards at an angle, shave the chocolate into curls. As long as the knife is held at a sloping angle the chocolate will curl into long cigarette shapes. Pick out the best shapes and place separately; broken shavings can be kept in a box. Store covered in a cool place, preferably the refrigerator.

To use: Chocolate curls look really delicious placed on top of chocolate gâteau that are plain-iced with chocolate icing. Try also on top of chocolate cup cakes. Pretty sprinkled over the tops of creamy desserts or sprinkled over ice-cream.

Glacé fruits

Glacé cherries and angelica are most suitable for decoration – other glacé fruit can be a little expensive. Glacé cherries can come in green and gold colours as well. Before using any glacé fruits, always wash off the sticky preserving syrup with warm water. Cherries may be cut in halves, quarters or they can also be finely chopped.

Angelica may also be chopped but is best cut into angelica leaves. To make these, first cut angelica into even strips about 5 mm–1 cm/¼–½ in wide. Then cut across at an angle to make diamond shapes. Arrange leaves and cherries together to make pretty designs.

To Use: Glacé cherry halves can be placed in the centre of prepared grapefruit halves or in melon wedges. Chopped glacé fruits look pretty stirred into canned fruit, particularly pears or peaches. Decorate meringue toppings on lemon pie or queen of puddings with angelica and cherries. Arrange pretty designs of both in the bases of jelly desserts so when turned out they appear on the top.

Using dried herbs and prepared seasonings

All herbs are different but nearly every one has an affinity with a certain food and it's important to use them where the flavours blend best. Dried herbs are stronger; they should be used in moderation and cannot be used as freely as fresh herbs.

When trying out herbs in recipes use not more than a good pinch – about ¼ level teaspoon for every 4 servings. Start with the more common ones and then later experiment with the more unusual ones. Store dried herbs in screw-topped jars, best kept away from the sunlight and remember dried herbs don't keep indefinitely.

Bay leaves

They have a pleasant aromatic taste and can be used very generally. They give a subtle flavour to any meat or chicken casserole and they may be added along with slices of lemon and parsley stalks to a liquor that fish is to be poached in.

Try boiling new potatoes for potato salad with a bay leaf and a peeled onion added to the water or when heating up milk for a white sauce, add a bay leaf and a small peeled onion stuck with a clove – allow milk to infuse for 15 minutes to get a good flavour. Always discard the bay leaf before serving any recipe.

Rosemary

This herb has a distinctive rather sweet flavour but use with care. It goes well with meat, in particular lamb or pork and can be used in moderation in fish, bacon and ham recipes. Dried rosemary is rather spiky like pine needles; if rubbing over the surface of a joint leave whole but where it is to be added to made-up dishes, crush or pound well before using.

Rub the fat on a leg of lamb or a joint of pork with salt and dried rosemary before roasting, or sprinkle crushed rosemary over lamb chops before grilling. Add a pinch crushed rosemary to an omelette mixture and serve with grilled bacon rashers and fried mushrooms.

Marjoram

A fragrant herb that has a sweet spicy flavour – it comes from the same family as oregano, a wild marjoram, with a stronger more pungent flavour. Oregano is used a great deal in Italian cookery and both are excellent in all veal dishes and added to mushroom or tomato recipes, in particular those for sauces or fillings.

Marjoram is a good herb to use in made-up meat dishes such as galantines, meat pies or even shepherd's pie. Try rubbing dried marjoram with a good seasoning of salt over the surface of a beef joint before roasting.

Thyme

Another herb with a distinctive flavour that should be used carefully and one that blends well with other herbs. Often used in stuffing with lemon or parsley or in stews or casseroles, particularly those made with chicken or veal and nice added to vegetable soups.

Thyme, bay leaf and parsley stalks are the main flavouring herbs used in a *bouquet garni*. Normally a fresh sprig of thyme is included but where dried thyme is used, tie the bay leaf and parsley stalks together in a bundle with a long thread and simply add a sprinkling of dried thyme to the recipe. Try blending a pinch crushed thyme with butter, and then add to any cooked new vegetables, particularly potatoes, carrots or peas before serving.

Basil
This has a hot clove-like flavour and is used a great deal in Italian cookery, where they add it to tomato, cheese, egg and fish recipes. Add a pinch of basil to a beef stew, especially if fresh or canned tomatoes are included in the recipe. Sprinkle basil over fresh halved tomatoes with oil and a seasoning of salt and pepper before grilling or crush into lemon juice and sprinkle over fried fish. Add a pinch to French dressing before pouring over sliced tomatoes and cucumber for a salad.

Sage
It has a very strong flavour and is excellent served with fatty or rich foods. For this reason in particular it is often used in stuffings for pork or goose and goes well in cheese dishes. It's surprisingly good in canned soups; try adding a pinch to tomato soup.

Tarragon
It has a mild aniseed flavour and is used a great deal in French cookery. Use mainly in sauces and especially good in cream sauces to be served over chicken or fish.

Parsley
This is a common herb with a mild flavour and can be used generally. Dried parsley cannot be used as a garnish, only as a flavouring but is good added to stews or casseroles where vegetables are included, in soups or added with butter to fresh cooked vegetables.

Bouquet garni or mixed herbs
A blend of bay leaf, marjoram, thyme, sage and parsley ready-mixed in the correct proportions. Best to use generally in soups,

stews or casseroles. Add a pinch to mushroom while frying, or any meat sauce.

Bouquet garni can be purchased in small bags with or without a long string attached. Use these in casseroles or stews especially beef, lamb or chicken recipes adding along with other ingredients, and if a string is attached tie this to the saucepan handle or allow to hang over the edge of the casserole. Just before serving, remove the bag by the string or fish out with a fork. The mixture of herbs in the bag can also be used for grilling or roasting; open the bag and rub a little of the herbs over the fish or meat to be grilled or roasted along with a little oil and salt.

Seasoned salts

There is a growing popularity for seasoned salts; they include celery, garlic and onion salt. Plain seasoning salt is a mixture of black pepper, salt, herbs and spices. They can be used in cooking or on the table sprinkled on chops, steak, hamburgers or cold meats. They are useful, too, for seasoning gravies.

Use to season flour for coating fish or chicken joints before frying; spice up oil and vinegar dressings; for seasoning soups, and over egg, cheese or vegetable salads. Try adding seasoned salt and lemon juice to melted butter and then pour over hot, newly cooked vegetables.

Garlic powder

This is very useful where a touch of garlic is needed but fresh garlic is not used. It can be used in meat or chicken casseroles or sprinkled over a leg of lamb before roasting. Try a little in salad dressing but use carefully.

Barbecue seasoning

It is a blend of spices including paprika, celery salt, garlic powder, nutmeg, cloves, black pepper and mustard powder. It can be added to bastes for grills and roasts or sprinkled over hot grilled meat before serving.

Salad dressing mixes

These are dry mixed seasonings that simply need to be added to oil, vinegar and water. They come in several flavours including French, Italian and garlic dressing mixes. To use, simply measure

4 tablespoons vinegar, 125 ml/¼ pint oil and 2 tablespoons water into a screw-topped jar, add the salad dressing mix, cover and shake well to mix. This larger quantity is useful to keep handy in the refrigerator; always shake well before using.

Index

Katie Stewart
The Times Cookery Book £3.50

Carefully chosen from the recipes published in *The Times* over the last few years and including many new ones, this collection of recipes by Katie Stewart is practical, varied and imaginative.

Selected to suit both everyday needs and special occasions, these recipes provide a rich source of new ideas for anyone who enjoys cooking.

Kathy Barnes
The Infra-Red Cook Book £1.50

The complete guide to infra-red cookery, the fast, clean, versatile and inexpensive method of cooking. This essential manual tells you the advantages of an infra-red grill and how to use it, plus a comprehensive series of mouth-watering recipes for all occasions, cooking frozen foods, cleaning and servicing, and a list of tried and tested models.

Marguerite Patten
Learning to Cook £2.50

A book which tells you how to cook easily and economically, serve simple, appetizing meals, and know which foods should be at their best in each month of the year. The author gives advice on choosing kitchen equipment, filling the store cupboard, and what to do if things go wrong. There are suggestions for using up leftovers and ideas for parties, picnics and Christmas. Keep this book handy — and your family contented!

Claire Loewenfeld and Philippa Back
Herbs for Health and Cookery £2.50

'Not just a cookery book but a fascinating compendium on herbs; as cures for a host of ailments, as refreshing drinks both alcoholic and "soft", as beauty aids, as used in diets and invalid cooking and as a sheer delight to have around the house' SCOTSMAN

Elisabeth Orsini
The Book of Pies £1.95

To prepare this veritable encyclopaedia of piecraft, Elisabeth Orsini has traced the pie back through history, discovering the immense variety of traditional pies and tarts that have graced the tables of cottage and castle with distinction. She has adapted over 200 recipes to suit today's cook, suggesting a mouthwatering variety of fillings and offering guidance on preparing the all-important pastry.

Theodora Fitzgibbon
A Taste of Ireland £3.95

This zestful welcome to the Emerald Isle is no orthodox cookery book, for the recipes are accompanied by a fascinating series of photographs, many of them over a hundred years old, and all a reminder of the vigorous life of nineteenth-century Ireland. Visitors have happily discovered Ireland's rich variety of delectable dishes. Theodora Fitzgibbon's selection draws from the flourishing tradition of Irish cooking, including many recipes from private family papers, never published before.

'More than just a cookery book ... a selection of the best of traditional Irish recipes and superb old Irish photographs' IRISH TOURIST BOARD

'A feast of a book' ULSTER TATLER

Gail Duff
Gail Duff's Vegetarian Cookbook £2.95

Vegetarian eating is economical as well as nutritious. Beans, pastas, rice, eggs, cheese, vegetable curries, salads and more allow plenty of scope for the most mouthwatering menus.

'Develops meatless eating into authentic cuisine' THE TIMES

'Really imaginative ... recipes anyone would be tempted to eat, vegetarian or not!' STANDARD

Rosemary Hume and Muriel Downes
The Best of Cordon Bleu £1.95

Rosemary Hume and Muriel Downes have run the Cordon Bleu Cookery School in London for many years. Their superb collection of recipes includes all the classic dishes that have been favourites with the students over the years — coquille St Jacques parisienne, sauté de porc mongroise, caramel mousse with caramel sauce and strawberries, and many more. There are menu suggestions for every occasion, from Sunday brunch parties to midsummer suppers. The perfect introduction to one of the world's great cuisines.

Jancis Robinson
Masterglass

a practical course in wine tasting £2.95

This is a book for all those who want to know more about wine, but already know that drinking it is much more interesting than reading about it. It explains how wine is made, what factors influence taste, and how to get every possible pleasure from drinking it. Side by side with all this necessary information is a practical course in developing tasting skills. *Masterglass* shows you how to drink your way to a real knowledge of wine.

Cook books

☐	**The Infra-Red Cook Book**	Kathy Barnes	£1.50p
☐	**The Microwave Cook Book**	Carol Bowen	£1.95p
☐	**Cooking on a Shoestring**	} Gail Duff	£1.95p
☐	**Vegetarian Cookbook**		£2.95p
☐	**Crockery Pot Cooking**	Theodora Fitzgibbon	£1.50p
☐	**The Book of Herbs**	Dorothy Hall	£1.75p
☐	**The Best of Cordon Bleu**	Rosemary Hume and Muriel Downes	£1.95p
☐	**Diet for Life**	Mary Laver and Margaret Smith	£1.95p
☐	**Quick and Easy Chinese Cooking**	Kenneth Lo	£1.95p
☐	**Herbs for Health and Cookery**	Claire Loewenfeld and Philippa Back	£2.50p
☐	**The Preserving Book**	Caroline Mackinlay	£4.50p
☐	**The Book of Pies**	Elisabeth Orsini	£1.95p
☐	**Learning to Cook**	Marguerite Patten	£2.50p
☐	**Traditional French Cooking**	Jennie Reekie	60p
☐	**Complete International Jewish Cookbook**	Evelyn Rose	£2.95p
☐	**Caribbean Cookbook**	Rita Springer	£1.75p
☐	**The Times Cookery Book**	} Katie Stewart	£2.95p
☐	**Shortcut Cookery**		£1.95p
☐	**Freezer Cookbook**	Marika Hanbury Tenison	£1.95p
☐	**The Pan Picnic Guide**	Karen Wallace	£1.95p
☐	**Mediterranean Cooking**	Paula Wolfert	£1.95p

Non-fiction

☐ **The Money Book**	Margaret Allen	£2.95p
☐ **Fall of Fortresses**	Elmer Bendiner	£1.75p
☐ **The British Way of Birth**	Catherine Boyd and Lea Sellers	£1.50p
☐ **100 Great British Weekends**	John Carter	£2.95p
☐ **Last Waltz in Vienna**	George Clare	£1.95p
☐ **Walker's Britain**	Andrew Duncan	£4.95p
☐ **Travellers' Britain**	Arthur Eperon	£2.95p
☐ **The Tropical Traveller**	John Hatt	£2.50p
☐ **The Lord God Made Them All**	James Herriot	£1.95p
☐ **The Neck of the Giraffe**	Francis Hitching	£2.50p
☐ **A Small Town is a World**	David Kossoff	£1.00p
☐ **Prayers and Graces**	Allen Laing illus. by Mervyn Peake	£1.25p
☐ **Kitchen & Bathroom Book**	Jose Manser	£5.95p
☐ **Best of Shrdlu**	Denys Parsons	£1.00p
☐ **Dipped in Vitriol**	Nicholas Parsons	£1.75p
☐ **The Bargain Book**	Barty Phillips	£1.95p
☐ **Thy Neighbour's Wife**	Gay Talese	£1.75p
☐ **Just off for the Weekend**	John Slater	£2.50p
☐ **Dead Funny**	Fritz Spiegl	£1.50p
☐ **The Third Wave**	Alvin Toffler	£2.75p
☐ **The World Atlas of Treasure**	Derek Wilson	£6.50p
☐ **Shyness**	Philip Zimbardo	£1.95p

All these books are available at your local bookshop or newsagent, or can be ordered direct from the publisher. Indicate the number of copies required and fill in the form below   9

....

Name..
(Block letters please)

Address..

....

Send to Pan Books (CS Department), Cavaye Place, London SW10 9PG
Please enclose remittance to the value of the cover price plus:
35p for the first book plus 15p per copy for each additional book ordered
to a maximum charge of £1.25 to cover postage and packing
Applicable only in the UK

While every effort is made to keep prices low, it is sometimes
necessary to increase prices at short notice. Pan Books reserve
the right to show on covers and charge new retail prices which
may differ from those advertised in the text or elsewhere